Reality of Money
and
The Federal Reserve

By Stephen Clark
and Frank Wallace

Direct inquiries and correspondence to:

Stephen Clark
P. O. Box 6100
Diamondhead, MS 39525

www.RealityofMoney.org

ISBN: 1450553397
ISBN-13: 9781450553391

Visit www.booksurge.com to order additional copies.

This is dedicated to the memory of Rosemary Wallace.

Acknowledgements and Gratitude to:

OMNI Publications
P.O. Box 9000566
Palmdale, CA, 93590-0566
For quotes from *The Federal Reserve
Conspiracy*, by Eustace Mullins; *The Green
Magicians*, by Thomas Porter; *Money
Creators*, by Gertrude Coogan

American Free Press
645 Pennsylvania Avenue SE
Suite 100,
Washington, D.C. 20003
Subscription price $59 one year, $99 for
two years, $17.76 for a 16-week "Get
Acquainted" subscription.
Call 1-888-699-NEWS toll free.
View *AFP On-Line* at www.
americanfreepress.net
For the quotes and cartoon illustrations
from the reprint of
"Billions for the Bankers, Debts for the
People," by Sheldon Emry

GSG &Associates Publishers
P.O. Box 590
San Pedro, CA 90733
Phone 310-548-3455
Fax 310-548-5802
For quotes from *Tragedy And Hope: A History of The World in Our Time,* by Carroll Quigley

Sheriar Foundation
807 34th Ave. S.
North Myrtle Beach, SC 29582
Phone: 843 272 1339
Fax: 843 361 1747
www.sheriarbooks.org
(Information on Avatar Meher Baba)
For Meher Baba's quotations

Peter Cook and Monetary Science
Publishing
Wickliffe, OH 44092

Jacques S. Jaikaran, MD, and
Glenbridge Publishing Ltd.,
19923 E. Long Ave.
Centennial, CO 80016
For quotes from *Debt Virus*

MEDIA BY-PASS MAGAZINE
Jim Thomas, P.O. Box 5326
Evansville, Indiana 47716
Phone: 812 477 8670
Fax: 812 477 8677
www.4bypass.com

Berret-Koehler Publishers, Inc.
235 Montgomery St., Suite 650
San Francisco, CA 94104-2916
For quotes from *Confessions of an Economic Hit Man*, by John Perkins
Copyright 2004 John Perkins.
All rights reserved.
www.bkconnection.com

Stephen Zarlenga, founder of the American Monetary Institute
P.O. Box 601
Valatie, NY 12184
www.Monetary.org
For quotes from The Quarterly Bulletin of *The American Money Scene*

Ontario Consultants
on Religious Tolerance
www.religioustolerance.org
For the Versions of The Golden Rule in twenty-one World Religions

Edward Bulwer Lytton 1839:

The pen is mightier than the sword, but the purse conquereth them both.

Aristotle, *Ethics* 1133:

Money exists not by nature but by law.

Media By-Pass Magazine:

America, Wake up! We have been conned with the BIG-LIE that we are Free People, when the fact is: We have become a nation of debt-shackled, "news controlled" tax slaves of a few privileged bankers who control most all legislation, commerce, and "national-news" in our country. And We Americans cannot get Free from this insidious entrapment... unless a majority of us awakens to this truth!

Henrik Ibsen:

Home life ceases to be free and beautiful as soon as it is founded on borrowing and debt.

Jesus, the Christ in the Gospel of St. John 8:32:

Know the truth and the truth shall set you free.

TABLE OF CONTENTS

"A nation can survive its fools, and even the ambitious. But it cannot survive treason from within. An enemy at the gates is less formidable, for he is known and carries his banner openly. But the traitor moves amongst those within the gate freely, his sly whispers rustling through all the alleys, heard in the very halls of government itself. For the traitor appears not a traitor; he speaks in accents familiar to his victims, and he wears their face and their garments. He appeals to the baseness that lies in the hearts of all men. He rots the soul of a nation. He works secretly and unknown in the night to undermine the pillars of the city. He infects the body politic, so that it can no longer resist. A murderer is less to fear."

Marcus Tullius Cicero, 42 BC

PREFACE

Frank Wallace:

There are many things more important than money:

God is more important than money.

Love is more important than money.

Moral right is more important than money.

Truth is more important than money.

Integrity is more important than money.

Honor is more important than money.

Compassion and concern for humanity are more important than money.

The factors that make civilized human beings are more important than money.

Our legacy as Americans is more important than money.

Our founders' vision for the American nation and the nation's citizens, indeed for humankind, is more important than money.

Universal freedom, peace, and prosperity are all more important than money.

"If a nation values anything more than free-dom, it will lose its freedom; and the irony of it is that if it is comfort or money that it values more, it will lose that too."

Somerset Maugham, 1941.

14

FOREWORD

What faces us all is a most important fundamental issue. As money today funds and controls and determines virtually everything that happens in this modern, increasingly digital financial world, we must ask, who morally, ultimately deserves to own the rights and benefits of money creation?

Morally, the choice is clear that ALL Americans deserve to benefit, not just the private banking cartels. Consider, how might our lives be monumentally different today with debt-free money for education, healthcare, infrastructure, and disaster relief instead of debt money for nearly a hundred years?

The private banking cartel owners of the cleverly misnamed Federal Reserve Bank, which successfully lobbied to get the Federal Reserve Act passed in 1913, remain the sole beneficiary of money usage. The brilliant idea to create and print money at will, and charge interest to any borrower, especially governments, has worked quite well for them and not so well for "We, the People." The bankers always win in any conflict, no matter which side prevails.

What is so wrong about the Federal Reserve? The "Fed" takes the credit of the American People, their most valuable asset, converts it into money, and then lends this money to the people, and their government as interest-bearing debt. Technically and morally, this is fraud. It is not too much to say that about 90% of the problems Americans struggle with politically can be traced back to using the morally wrong private bankers' money system instead of debt-free money provided for in the Constitution. It is abusive and criminal.

Thanks to its monopoly granted by Congress, the Fed routinely writes uncovered checks, on no bank account anywhere, and the government honors them. If you or I wrote a check with no money in the bank to cover it, we would be put in jail. When the Fed writes checks, it is creating money. In other words, the Fed gets its inventory, money, for free. It is the only business in America that does. **The Fed rules America.**

To right this basic moral wrong, we must demand that Congress restore the right of money creation, and its benefits, to the American people, where it truly belongs. "We, the People," allowed an irresponsible Congress to relinquish this authority, and we need to reverse it for any real hope of things to get truly better for all Americans. It is long overdue. The facts given in this work are easily verified. The rest is our opinion.

Stephen Clark

"Throughout history, periods of high moral attainment have been periods of sound money, while periods of moral disintegration have followed the debasement of the monetary unit. Fiat money, printing press money, or money without intrinsic value is dishonest money, and the moral laws having been violated, moral degradation is inevitable."

Howard E. Kershner, Gold, God, and Government, as quoted in Gold Newsletter, March, 1988.

INTRODUCTION

This book was written because its authors disdain unfairness, injustice, abuse of power, totalitarianism, and tyranny. The important information presented here is for the "common man," the constantly struggling "middle class," and all "Main Street" Americans who work, produce, pay legal taxes, obey laws, and instill civilizing values in their children.

Our third president, Thomas Jefferson, said it best:

I have sworn on the Altar of God eternal hostility against every form of tyranny over the minds of man.

We humbly ask the reader to assimilate and grasp this sordid story of man's inhumanity to man as it relates to our monetary system's complete control by private bankers. **It is a story of what the powerful few continue to do to the not-fully-informed many.** The information presented here is the key to economic freedom as citizens of a sovereign nation so that "We, the People," can cease being economic slaves of the banking industry. **We have carelessly let our precious heritage, given by the wisdom of our great Founding Fathers, be taken from us.** We pray that decent and responsible Americans will unite in political action to regain our heritage.

You will not find the information presented here in any other one place. Because most Americans have not seen it, several quotations are repeated for emphasis. We do not ask anyone to take our word that these facts are true. What we do ask is for anyone who is concerned with the best interests of family, their children, grandchildren, and our country, to do the research and make his or her own decisions. The truth as given here is easily verified, as readers will see that many researchers and authors have already exposed this moral wrong in the various publications cited.

In many respects, our country is in the biggest mess it has ever been in morally, economically, financially, and socially. No matter how earnestly concerned Americans work to correct what is wrong, they cannot be fully successful until we all have honest money and sound banking practices.

This can be a reality as soon as the citizens of America awaken to the error of the unwise choice that was made so long ago. It is not too late to remedy our economic situation if we collectively choose to hold our representatives to the original provisions of the Constitution. Refuse to elect anyone who does not recognize the error of the Federal Reserve Act, which does such grievous harm to so many, and elect only those who will vow to uphold the principles given in the Constitution.

If our nation is to be saved from eventual bankruptcy, it will be because enough Americans understand political and economic reality in time to take political action.

The Biloxi, Mississippi, newspaper *The Sun Herald*, published on July 6, 2003, an article by Jay Ambrose under the heading "Federal Spending is Totally Out of Control" on the editorial opinion page, followed by a tabulation of the national debt from 1791 to 2002, which was then (2002) at 6 trillion, 228 billion, 235 million, 965 thousand, and 597 dollars! In 1791, it was just over $75,000. Now, in 2008 it is over $9 trillion! The source was the BUREAU OF THE PUBLIC DEBT IN THE TREASURY DEPARTMENT.

Too many good Americans, millions, have worked, fought, and died to let citizens continue to be run by the banking industry. The only thing that will correct this quagmire is to use common sense and political power to end the bankers' insidious rule. It will not be easy, but it is necessary for the best interests and well-being of all Americans.

We wish to say from the onset that commercial banking is an indispensable part of our economic structure, but our current Federal Reserve banking system is NOT indispensable. It can be easily proven to have actively waged economic warfare against the American people since its inception in 1913 when an ill-informed and irresponsible Congress turned against the American people and passed the Federal Reserve Act in favor of the banking industry.

This is not intended to be an attack on the banking industry, but it is pro-America and pro-"We, the People." Most of the people who work for banks are good people, just engaged in earning a living. The "friendly local banker" just knows that banking is a good business to be in. We respect the banking industry's economic power, but it is morally wrong that it should have the degree of political power that is reserved in the Constitution for "We, the People." Most Americans have been kept so busy trying to earn a living to provide for their families, they have not studied, and thus, do not understand the concepts of the power of money creation.

The main point of this work is to convince the reader (enough to inspire action) that the power of money creation needs to remain within governmental control of Congress under the US Treasury if the government is to regain and retain its sovereignty. When that power is turned over or delegated to private interests, the nation degenerates into corruption, as is evidenced in every quadrant of society one cares to look into. Basing a monetary system in commodities, lorded over by private interests rather than by law administered by accountability, quickly accelerates the concentration of power into the hands of a plutocracy, thus, destroying all possibility of social justice. This is our political and economic reality today.

AMERICAN FREE PRESS October 2001

24

INJUSTICE BEGINS:
WHAT WENT WRONG

From the earliest days of our country, there has been a built-in conflict between the owners of capital and the vast majority of the people who live off their ability to work each day. Each group has sought legislation favorable to its interests.

From the very beginning, our first president, George Washington, had to balance the money-elite banker factions with the "We, the People" factions. Though the first treasury secretary, Alexander Hamilton, was one of the aristocratic banker elitists, the task fell to him to organize the various opposing interests. His early efforts evolved into what has now become our current two-party political system. Hamilton was killed in 1804 in a duel with Vice President Aaron Burr, a member of the opposing party that denounced the aristocracy. Could money issues have been a cause of the animosity?

President Washington had a wise foreign policy:

Friendly relations with all nations; special relations with none.

It did not endure, for it, and other provisions of our Constitution, have been gradually, but surely captured and subverted to unfairly benefit the banker elitists.

The harmful effects of monetary power are plain for all in the world to see and feel.

Our second president, John Adams, said:

...all the perplexities, confusion, and distress in America arise, not from defects in their Constitution or Confederation, not from want of honor or virtue, so much as from the downright ignorance of the nature of coin, credit and circulation.

The ink was hardly dry on the Constitution when the banking industry began reaching for its power. This attempt caused Thomas Jefferson to proclaim:

Already a money aristocracy has set the government at defiance...**I believe that banks are more dangerous to our liberties than standing armies. If the American people ever allow private banks to control the issue of money, first by inflation, then by deflation, the banks and corporations that will grow up around them (the banks), will deprive the people of their property until their children will wake up homeless on the continent their fathers conquered.**

Through the years, laws favorable to the banking industry gradually reduced the power of the people. One of the best known was the National Banking Act of 1863. An Ohio banker, Mr. John Sherman, who was also a federal senator, wrote to the Rothschild brothers in London about the profits to be made under the new Act, notwithstanding the fact that it gives the national banks almost absolute control of the national finance. Sherman wrote:

The few who can understand the system will either be so interested in its profits, or so dependent upon its favors, that there will be no opposition from that class, while on the other hand, the great body of people mentally incapable of comprehending the tremendous advantages that capital (bankers) derives from the system, will bear its burden without complaint and perhaps without even suspecting that the system is inimical to their interests.

This statement is extremely offensive to anyone. You should be truly offended to know that bankers consider that "We, the People" are mentally incapable of understanding the system. It is infuriating to these writers and is an insult to our intelligence, and the intelligence of all responsible and thinking Americans.

Consider now, two equally offensive quotes that reveal the selfish motives of the private owners and operators of the central banks in the United States and, indeed, now the world.

Amshel Meyer Rothschild:

Permit me to issue and control the money of a nation, and I care not who makes its laws.

This arrogant statement by the founder of the Rothschild European banking dynasty in the 1700s is perfect to introduce the reader to the purpose of this treatise because it goes straight to the heart of the matter of what is wrong with our current corrupt and dysfunctional government. Rothschild eventually succeeded in his quest to dominate and control the economy, and thus, most of the population of our nation. This is the situation in the United States today, and coming from the "horse's mouth," it makes our case. If the private creation of money is superior to law, and by current law, it is, we need to change the law from the PRIVATE to PUBLIC creation of money as Article I, Section 8, of the Constitution provides. The quote reveals accurately the mindset of the banking elite, who with their cartels and supporters in Congress were eventually successful in accomplishing this goal with the passage in 1913 of the Federal Reserve Act in Congress.

From that time forward to now, because of this selfish and destructive act and its supporting evil companion, the Federal Income Tax Bill, also introduced in 1913, America has degenerated needlessly and tragically into a land of poverty and misery for millions of its citizens.

The Federal Income Tax Bill was never ratified by the majority of states at the time in the 16th Amendment of the Constitution and is, therefore, illegal though still enforced through tactics of fear and intimidation. But the 16th Amendment, whether ratified or not, is beside the point because its passage conferred no new right of taxation powers to Congress.

Longtime patriot activist and constitutional advocate Devvy Kidd reported in a November 18, 2005, *WorldNetDaily* exclusive commentary on the World Wide Web/Internet that her friend, Bill Benson, holds 17,000 court-certified documents that prove beyond any doubt that the 16th Amendment was never ratified. This amendment to the Constitution, supported by compromised federal judges, helps to defraud the American people of the fruit of their labors via the income tax.

The individual income tax on earnings from our "labor" has been immorally and illegally collected from

Americans since 1913. A January 15, 1984, Grace Commission report by President Ronald Reagan's impaneled committee to find ways of cutting government spending, found that all of the collected "income tax" goes totally to pay the interest on the national debt. None of our income tax money goes to run the government to benefit education, health care, infrastructure building and maintenance, or to disaster relief, although there is no reason not to do so under the Constitution. All of the individual income taxes from the "labor" portion of the many and varied taxes, fees, licenses, etc. go to the private bankers who were the architects of the plan, and who use it to fund all their wars, which place both victors and vanquished into debt to them.

Moreover, the Supreme Court has consistently ruled that **a God-given "right" cannot be taxed.** God has given all of us the "right" to the fruits of our labor, but the two-pronged subversion of our Constitution by the banking elite has been stealing the fruits of our labor in the form of the income tax since 1913 through the illegal taxing of individual income.

Title 26 of the United States Tax Code details and specifies the activities that can be taxed as income. It specifies alcohol, tobacco, foreign earnings, and certain corporate activities. These are the only things in the tax code that are subject to an income tax. **Morally, the fruits of our labor, our personal and individual income, should never be taxed.**

Later, in 1933, the bankers who adopted and perpetuated this mode of economic control privately circulated a statement that revealed their true aims. Our second quote, which is a prime example of the harmful mentality of the bankers, became known to the public as **"The Bankers' Manifesto."** It was first published in *THE ORGANIZER*, the January Civil Servants Yearbook, and in the *NEW AMERICAN* of February 1934. The more recent *Monetary Science Publications* version, "Bankernomics in One Easy Lesson," represents succinctly how the keepers of the Federal Reserve Banks feel about "We, the People."

Capital (bankers) must protect itself (themselves) in every way, through combination (organization) and through legislation. Debts must be collected and loans and mortgages foreclosed as soon as possible. When through a process of law the common people have lost their homes, they will be more tractable (docile) and more easily governed by the strong arm of the law, applied by the central power of wealth, under the control of leading financiers. People without homes will not quarrel with their leaders. This is well known

among our principal men now engaged in forming an imperialism of capital (bankers) to govern the world. By dividing the people (into Democrats, Republicans, conservatives, liberals, socialists, etc.) we can get them to expend their energies in fighting over questions of no importance to us except as teachers of the common herd. Thus, by discrete action, we can secure for ourselves what has been generally planned and successfully accomplished.

How does this make you feel? Note: "...teachers of the common herd." Note also: "...forming an imperialism of capital (bankers) to govern the world Have you heard of "The New World Order"?

In *Tragedy and Hope: A History of the World In Our Time,* Carroll Quigley cites its objectives:

...nothing less than a world wide system of financial control in private hands able to dominate the political systems of each country and the economy of the world as a whole.

The conspiring bankers may have succeeded beyond their wildest dreams when they subverted the Constitution early in the last century. Observe the state of the world today. The superrich have certainly gotten richer, and the world's poor are even poorer, thanks to the enacted central banking policies. These two extremely offensive quotes are reason enough that the authors hope to awaken the public through this exposé to stir an overwhelming public demand that our Congress persons and Senators restore the Congress and the White House to the provisions in the original Constitution in order to benefit all American citizens and not just the bankers and their partner associates.

Members of the Money Power are largely unknown to the public but their legmen/front men (and women), are all too visible in government, national and international corporations, media, universities, foundations, some churches, and in such organizations as the Council on Foreign Relations, and the Trilateral Commission. European counterpart semisecret organizations are The Royal Institute of International Affairs and The Club of Rome. Under the guise of aiding nations, all do a round-table dance with the United Nations to disenfranchise the disadvantaged throughout the world through debt. The Money Powers regularly get together at the Bilderbergers' meetings and other private conferences around the world. It is at secret meetings like this that the "real" policies are discussed and planned for the rest of us, long before they get to Congress, the Senate, and the White House.

In mainstream America, a group referred to variously as the "Elite Minority," the "Political Nation," the "Establishment," the "System," or "The Man" comprises the people so strategically entrenched and powerful that they simply run things without the informed consent of American citizens. The private owners of the "Fed" rule America because they, through gradual infiltration, rule the agencies, official or otherwise, of most organizations, the major corporations, and media today.

John Perkins exposed the inner workings of these intertwined groups when he wrote *Confessions of an Economic Hit Man*, as a dedication to two foreign presidents who were assassinated because they opposed the fraternity of bankers, corporations, and government whose goal is global empire. More details appear in his sequel, *The Secret History of the American Empire: Economic Hit Men, Jackals, and the Truth about Global Corruption*. In *Confessions*, Perkins, a self-admitted former "economic hit man" (EHM), reveals the existence and the job descriptions of such individuals. With the permission of the publisher of *Confessions of an Economic Hit Man*, we reprint John Perkins' description of his job:

...To encourage world leaders to become part of a vast network that promotes US commercial interests. In the end, **these leaders become ensnared in a web of debt that ensures their loyalty**. We can draw on them whenever we desire to satisfy our political, economic, or military needs. In turn, they bolster their political positions by bringing industrial parks, power plants, and airports to their people. The owners of US engineering/construction companies become fabulously wealthy.

According to Perkins, EHMs basically work to produce economic growth studies that justify huge international loans that in turn funnel the money to US companies such as Bechtel, Halliburton, Brown & Root, Stone & Webster, and others through mega-engineering projects. Then, through tactics of intimidation, threats, and payoffs, EHMs work to bankrupt the countries receiving the loans so that they will forever be beholden to their creditors. The net result is to create huge profits for the contractors, while making a very few influential and wealthy families in the foreign countries even wealthier with no consequence to them if the debt burden also deprives most of a country's citizenry of education, health, and rudimentary social services.

From the preface of *Confessions of an Economic Hit Man*, John Perkins writes:

"Economic Hit Men" (EHMs) are highly paid professionals who cheat countries around the globe out of trillions of dollars. They funnel money from the World Bank, the US Agency for International Development (USAID), and other foreign "aid" organizations into the coffers of huge corporations and the pockets of a few wealthy families who control the planet's natural resources. Their tools include fraudulent financial reports, rigged elections, payoffs, extortion, sex, and murder. They play a game as old as empire, but one that has taken on new and terrifying dimensions during this time of globalization. I should know; I was an EHM.

President Eisenhower, in his historic January 1961 farewell address to the nation, warned the American people of the dangers to come if the citizenry did not remain vigilant over the government:

In the councils of government, we must guard against the acquisition of unwarranted influence, whether sought or unsought, by the military-industrial complex. The potential for the disastrous rise of misplaced power exists, and will persist. We must never let the weight of this combination endanger our liberties or democratic processes. We should take nothing for granted. Truly an alert and knowledgeable citizenry can compel the proper meshing of the huge industrial and military machinery of defense with our peaceful methods and goals, so that security and liberty may prosper together.

It is imperative for all Americans to demand monetary reform from their legislators and compel them to pass a new law that empowers "We, the People," with debt-free money for national business, to educate our people, to treat their illnesses and problems, and build and maintain our national infrastructure. Let us remove the power from the banker cartels and restore it to a Congress that truly has the best interests of the people at heart. This would allow the hope of fulfillment of "the American Dream" for "ordinary" people. Anything less is a continuing shame, both for those who choose to exploit others for personal gain and for those who will not awaken and take the rightful power granted them in the Constitution.

There is no good reason for anyone to lose his or her home going bankrupt over medical bills. There is also no good reason that our college graduates must start life saddled with $50,000 debt as a reward for getting an education. **The fact that Americans find themselves in these situations constitutes a national tragedy and is a travesty.** We must recognize that shelter is a paramount need of the people. Shelter is not a luxury and should never be subject to arbitrary market forces unfairly controlled by greedy bankers. Loans for homes should be made at a reasonable rate of less than **6% or even less at simple interest.** When, through no fault of their own, such as natural disasters, homeowners cannot make the payments, Christian and all other universal spiritual, moral principles dictate nothing less than the total forgiving of the debt. Charging interest at more than a reasonable rate, ballooning or adjustable rates, and other deliberately confusing mortgage contracts should be considered criminal and made unlawful. We cannot much longer sustain a monetary system where, by (immoral) law the relatively few are made enormously wealthy by the misfortunes of many others.

A wealth of information on the subject of monetary reform was published in *The Green Magicians*, a wonderful little 1968 book by author Thomas A. Porter. In the book, Porter writes about Congressman Charles A. Lindbergh Sr., father of the famous flyer, who is said to have been the only congressman who read the entire Federal Reserve Act. This information is verified in

Lindbergh's own book, *Lindbergh on the Federal Reserve* (formerly entitled *The Economic Pinch*). Porter gives an account of Lindbergh's reactions and quotations in the Minority Report of its original hearing:

It violates every principle of popular Democratic Representative Government and every declaration of the Democratic Party and platform pledges from Thomas Jefferson down to the beginning of this Congress... It recognizes the superior sovereignty of the embodied institution of money over any power of the government so that neither the government, in its sovereign capacity, nor the people nor their representatives can initiate the placement of one dollar of monetary functionary into actual exchange among the people except through the agency of organized money loaners with purely selfish interests...The Glass Bill (Federal Reserve Bank Act) positively abolishes the United States Treasury and public money of the people and substitutes the so-called Federal Reserve Banks, which by the term of the Bill are to be the exclusive stock of the bankers. **It reduces the people's Treasury Department and the Bureau of Printing and Engraving**

**to the position of a job printing house
for the private use of bankers.**

Aristotle, in *Aristotle, On Man in the Universe, Politics* wrote:

And we have found the answer to our original question, whether the art of wealth-getting is the business of the manager of a household and of the statesman, or is not their business. It is an art which is of primary importance to them. As political science does not make men, but takes them from nature and uses them, so nature provides them with food from the elements of earth, air, or sea. But at this stage begins the duty of the manager of a household, who has to order the things which nature supplies. He may be compared to the weaver, who had not to make, but to use wool, and to know what sort of wool is good and serviceable or bad and unserviceable...Of the two sorts of wealth-getting one, as I have just said is a part of household management, the other is commerce. The former is necessary and honorable, the latter a kind of exchange which is justly censured;

for it is unnatural, and a mode by which men gain from one another. The most hated sort, and with the greatest reason, is **usury** (interest), which makes a gain out of money itself, and not from the natural use of it...**For money was intended to be used in exchange, but not to increase at interest**. And the term "interest," which means the birth of money from money is applied to the breeding of money because the offspring resembles the parent. Wherefore of all modes of making money this is the most unnatural.

A commentary on the above text by editor Louise Ropes Loomis, *Aristotle, On Man in the Universe* says:

The use of money as a standard of value and medium of exchange, as already explained, was to Aristotle its natural use. But the use of money as capital, especially the loaning of it at interest to get more money, a practice increasingly common in his time, seemed to him quite unnatural and wrong. Money was not a live thing. It did not naturally multiply, like flocks and herds.

Peter Cook makes the distinction between usury and (common) interest in his 1997 pamphlet *AWESOME POWERS OF: BANK DEPOSIT MONEY,* a Monetary Science Publication:

> Third world poverty and hunger [are] not born, but made by way of Capitalism's money and banking systems... it's time to review a little ancient and some recent history of Capitalism (less offensive name for Bankerism). What is known as Capitalism in our day was practiced over 4,000 years ago. However, such practice then was not known as Capitalism, but was known as **usury**. Usury was historically and biblically associated with the crimes of bloodshedding and murder. In the reign of King James I (1600), his Attorney General Noy stated: "Usurers are well ranked with murderers." The Jewish Encyclopedia, Vol. II, Apocrypha – Banash, quoting Ezekiel of the Bible referring to usurers: "He (the usurer) shall surely suffer death, his blood is upon him." It is important to understand that **usury and common interest are not the same thing**. Usu-

ry is a recondite money-creator's collateral-harvesting system, cultivated via the compound interest on debts. The common interest is equivalent to rent and often beneficial to society and commerce. Usury, better known in our day as Capitalism, is a Deposit (checkbook) Money Creator's debt-management mechanism, reconditely used in the concentration of wealth and resources of a nation into fewer and fewer hands...

The struggle for financial and political power continued until 1913. The bankers then achieved complete control with the passage of the Federal Reserve Banking Act, which took effect in 1914. The mechanism was now in place to control American interest rates and make a fortune lending the government fiat money at interest. To complete the plan, they also introduced the Federal Income Tax Bill in 1913 to ensure an endless supply of funds for the government to pay the interest on the ever-increasing national debt. To become law, the 16th Amendment to the Constitution was written, but needed ratification by at least thirty-six states. Only two states agreed to the plan, but the then secretary of state, Mr. Flanders Knox, simply announced that the required majority was achieved, and he was not questioned or challenged. To this day, the federal income tax is illegal, but is enforced all the same.

Adding salt to the grievous wound, **all collected income tax money goes to pay the interest on our national debt, and not to fund education, health and welfare, or for infrastructure.** The far-reaching effects of this most destructive act have inevitably led to the reality of our present situation.

With the intent of establishing a government free of European money control and influence, statesmen with Christian values wrote into the Constitution:

Congress shall have the Power to Coin Money and Regulate the Value Thereof.

Roger E. Elletson comments on this all important provision in the March 1985 Bulletin: *Legacy To The Victims of Corporate America:*

> It is the Federal Reserve that controls the Federal Government by controlling the government's purse strings. **The Federal Government is supposed to be the Sovereign power of a nation, but it is, in reality, just another debtor of the international bankers; a situation that completely usurps the**

powers granted to Congress under Article I, Section 8.5 of the Constitution of the United States that states, " ...Congress shall have the Power ... to Coin Money and Regulate the Value Thereof." We do not owe the National Debt to ourselves, as We, the People, are generally taught. We owe it to the bankers who have created it in terms of their **usurious monetary laws**.

Nowhere in this wonderful and precious document does it say for Congress to give away the supreme power of money creation and its benefits to private interests, yet this is exactly what happened so long ago during the Christmas holidays when most legislators were not present during the vote. Conceived by extremely selfish, greedy, and evil-minded men, The Federal Reserve Act was the worst Christmas present ever given to the American people.

The unwise passage of the Federal Reserve Act was nothing less than a national tragedy because through the original Constitution, Congress is morally obligated to provide every American citizen with **DEBT-FREE** (interest-free) money for education, health care, the building and maintenance of infrastructure, and disaster relief and repairs. Though not explicitly stated in this manner in the Constitution, we can rationally and correctly infer the founding founder's intent by answering the moral question: Who should benefit from America's monetary system? The choice is between ALL Americans or the relative few who own the private banking cartels. The fact that our ever growing so-called national debt that is now impossible to pay off is clear evidence that Congress made the wrong choice long ago. Just think of all the jobs that spending created money into circulation as intended instead of loaning money with interest into circulation would create!

Under the current system, ALL money issued is by design either debt or credit money, which unfairly gives the owners and associates of the central banks complete control of even our elected officials, including the Supreme Court and The White House.

In banking today, **DEBT = PROFIT.** The Money Creators wield absolute power to influence and pay off our current thoroughly corrupted Senate and House of Representatives. Lobbyist-influenced and bribed officials continue to increase our national debt to the point where **it is mathematically impossible to pay off!** Most of our citizens are now forced into an economic slavery of one form or another, and unless "We, the People," rise up and demand freedom from these economic shackles through honest representatives who are held accountable, the central bank owners will gradually claim ownership of everything under a totalitarian system. They are already well on their way.

It is necessary and entirely possible to regain an honest money system for America. Our constitutional legacy includes countless decent and responsible Americans who followed the wisdom of our Founding Fathers and built this nation. The guidelines were set by Thomas Paine, Patrick Henry, Benjamin Franklin, George Washington, John Adams, Thomas Jefferson, and others who were courageous enough to throw off the oppressive yoke of British Colonialism by authoring and signing the Constitution.

Our founders, to their everlasting glory, put in place a constitutional system that has brought great benefit to much of humankind. Many nations have benefited from America's generosity because of the work of good people who produce and deliver.

The lack of public knowledge about money has enabled the banking industry to prevail politically. It should not be this way and does not have to be. Even though the banking interests continually attempted to get laws passed in their favor from our nation's inception onward, **The United States had a constitutional money system from its founding until 1913, when the Federal Reserve Act was passed.**

The cleverly named "Fed," as it is called, is a blatant deception. The Federal Reserve is no more "Federal" than FedEx, the well-known delivery company. The Fed is not now and has never been a public agency, but IS a private cartel of bankers with international connections.

The Fed was planned and had its origins in November 1910 during an extended weeklong meeting (ten days) at J.P. Morgan's private estate on Jekyll Island off the Georgia coast. The conspirator participants were Senator Nelson W. Aldrich and bankers from the Rockefeller-Morgan-Rothschild-Harriman cartels. This group traveled in secret and called each other by their first names only. They dismissed the regular employees and servants at the Jekyll Island Club, and replaced them with new people who would not know any of them. Their excursion was disguised as a hunting trip, even though they had no guns or fishing equipment, and carried only briefcases and wore expensive suits.

It was during this secret meeting that the plan for a central bank, The Federal Reserve system, was created and written to introduce to the Congress. These people did not then have the best interests of the American people at heart, and due to their enacted policies, the nation is now in economic dire straits and many needlessly continue to suffer.

Paul Warburg, a lobbyist representing Rothschild interests, was paid $500,000 in 1910 dollars to lead the group and then lobby the proposed Act through Congress. He called the finished product "a banker's bank." He said:

This is your bank. Use it for your purposes.

There was no mention of any concern for the well-being of the American people. Warburg became the first Federal Reserve director of its Board of Governors.

The author of *The Creature From Jekyll Island,* G. Edward Griffin cites Anthony Sutton revealing Warburg's agenda in *Wall Street and FDR:*

Warburg's revolutionary plan to get American Society to go to work for Wall Street was astonishingly simple. Even today…academic theoreticians cover their blackboards with meaningless equations, and the general public struggles in bewildered confusion with inflation and the coming credit collapse, while the quite simple explanation of the problem goes un-discussed and almost entirely un-comprehended. **The Federal Reserve System is a legal private monopoly of the money**

supply operated for the benefit of the few under the guise of protecting and promoting the public interest.

One of the coconspirators, present at the meeting, Mr. Frank Vanderlip of the National City Bank, said many years later in *The Saturday Evening Post* (February 9, 1935):

Despite my views about the value to society of greater publicity for the affairs of corporations, there was an occasion near the close of 1910, when I was as secretive—indeed as furtive—as any conspirator...our secret expedition to Jekyll Island as the occasion of the actual conception of what eventually became the Federal Reserve System.

Perhaps he finally had an attack of conscience like former "economic hit man" John Perkins.

Senator Aldrich of Rhode Island was an investment associate of J.P. Morgan and had extensive holdings in banking, manufacturing, and public utilities. He was the Republican whip in the Senate, and was the chairman of the National Monetary Commission. Senator Aldrich was also the father-in-law to John D. Rockefeller Jr. His grandson, Nelson Aldrich Rockefeller, would in time become the vice-president of the United States.

The other participants in the banking conspiracy plan carried out at Jekyll Island are named and identified in *The Federal Reserve Conspiracy*, by Eustace Mullins, and in *The Creature from Jekyll Island, by G. Edward Griffin*. A government official accompanying Senator Aldridge was A. Piatt Andrew, the assistant secretary of the US Treasury at the time.

The representatives of the banking interests present at Jekyll Island were Frank Vanderlip, the president of the National City Bank of New York, who represented William Rockefeller and Kuhn–Loeb banking and Rockefeller Oil interests; Henry P. Davidson, a senior partner in the J.P. Morgan Co. Bank; Charles D. Norton, president of the J.P. Morgan Co., First National City Bank of New York; Benjamin Strong, head of the J.P. Morgan Bankers Trust Company, and later head of the Federal Reserve System; and lastly, Paul Moritz Warburg, a partner in Kuhn–Loeb & Co. banking of New York, who represented both the Rothschild brothers and the Warburgs' banking dynasty in Europe.

According to Thomas Porter in *The Green Magicians*, the Warburgs of the Warburg banking family in Europe, and the Rothschilds, through Jacob

Schiff, an agent in the United States, financed the Russian Revolution of 1917.

> Jacob Schiff was sent to the United States by the Rothschilds to gain financial control of the United States after the Rothschilds failed to win complete control in the Civil War. He succeeded and brought Paul M. Warburg to the United States from Germany in 1906 to help establish a central banking system. Warburg guided the writing of the Federal Reserve Act, became a citizen in 1911, and was appointed vice-chairman of the new Federal Reserve Board in 1914. **The leading bankers of the world financed the Russian Revolution**, not as a loan or a financial investment, but as their own cause.

In 1857, The prime minister of England, Benjamin Disraeli, addressed the Rothschild families gathered at the wedding of Lenora Rothschild to her cousin Alfonso. Thomas Porter gives the quote in *The Green Magicians:*

> Under this roof are the heads of the family of Rothschild, a name famous in every capital in Europe and ev-

ery division of the globe. **If you like, we shall divide the United States into two parts, one for you, James, and one for you, Lionel.** Napoleon will do exactly and all that I shall advise him, and to Bismarck will be suggested such an intoxicating program as to make him our abject slave.

Eustace Mullins stated that under Benjamin Strong, the Federal Reserve was brought into "interlocking relations" with the heads of the banks of England and France. Interestingly, Strong later died suddenly while in the midst of a 1928 congressional investigation into secret meetings where allegedly, the Fed governors met with the European Central Bankers to plan the Great Depression.

The entire sordid story of the Great Depression is documented in *The Creature From Jekyll Island: A Second Look at the Federal Reserve* by G. Edward Griffin. It is also well documented in *The Federal Reserve Conspiracy* by Eustace Mullins, *in The Federal Reserve Hoax: The Age Of Deception by Wickliffe B. Vennard Sr.,* ...*And The Truth Shall Set You Free* by David Icke, and in *Rule By Secrecy* by Jim Marrs. It is also well documented by researchers in various other works.

From the founding of the United States until 1913, we had a constitutional money system that was simple. Anyone who could read could understand it. Government-issued debt-free money was injected into the money stream for public purposes and for the public good. When, and only when, the nation's production increased, additional debt-free money was issued. A stable balance of money and national production was maintained to conduct the nation's business.

Abraham Lincoln, besieged by the private banking interests, had this to say about them:

The money power preys upon the nation in times of peace and conspires against it in times of adversity.

The wise words of Lincoln, popularly known as "Honest Abe," are timeless in that they describe the kind of honest money system America badly needs today. The following paragraph, from *The Conquest of Poverty* by Gerald G. McGeer, is an abstract of Senate Document 23, which details Lincoln's monetary system and was certified as correct by the Legislative Reference Service of the Library of Congress.

Money is the creature of law and the creation of the original issue of

money should be maintained as an exclusive monopoly of national government. Money possesses no value to the State other than given to it by circulation. Capital has its proper place and is entitled to every protection. The wages of man should be recognized in the structure of and in the social order as more important than the wages of money. **No duty is more imperative on the government than the duty it owes the people to furnish them with a sound and uniform currency and of regulating the circulation of the medium of exchange so that labor will be protected from a vicious currency, and commerce will be facilitated by cheap and safe exchanges.** The available supply of gold and silver being wholly inadequate to permit the issue of coins of intrinsic value of paper currency convertible into coin in the volume required to serve the needs of the people, some other basis for the issue of currency must be developed to prevent fluctuations in the value of paper money (currency) or any other substitute for money of intrinsic value that may come into use. The **monetary needs** of increasing numbers of people advancing towards higher standards of living **can and should be met by the government**. Such needs can be served by the issue of national currency and credit through the operation of a National Bank System. The circulation of a medium of exchange issued and backed by the government can be properly circulated and redundancy of issue avoided by withdrawing from circulation such amounts as may be necessary by taxation, re-deposited and otherwise. **The government has the power to regulate the currency and credit of a nation. Government should stand behind the currency and credit and the bank deposits of a nation. No individual should suffer a loss of money through depreciation, or inflated currency, or bankruptcy.** Government possessing the power to create and issue currency and credit as money and enjoying the right to withdraw both currency and credit from circulation by taxation and otherwise, need not and should not borrow capital at interest as the means of financing governmental work—and public enterprise. **The government should create, issue, and circulate all the currency and credit needed to satisfy the spending power of the government and the buying power of the consumers.** The privilege of creating and issuing money is not only the supreme prerogative of government, but it is government's greatest creative opportunity. By adoption of these principles, the long felt wait for a uniform medium of exchange will be satisfied. The taxpayer will be saved immense sums of interest, discounts, and exchanges. The financing of all public enterprise, the maintenance of stable government and ordered progress, and the conduct of the Treasury will become matters of practical administration. The people will be furnished with a currency as safe as their government. **Money will cease to be master and become the servant of humanity, and democracy will rise superior to the money power**...The Money Power preys upon the nation in times of peace and conspires against it in times of adversity. It is more despotic than Monarchy, more insolent than Aristocracy, more selfish than Bureaucracy. It denounces as public enemies, all who question its methods, or throw light upon its crimes.

President Lincoln, after the passage of the National Banking Act of 1863, prophesied and warned the American citizens:

I see in the future a crisis approaching that unnerves me and causes me to tremble for the safety of my country. Corporations have been enthroned, an era of corruption in high places will follow, and the money power of the country will endeavor to prolong its reign by working upon the prejudices of the people, until the wealth of the nation is aggregated in a few hands, and the Republic is destroyed.

The money power concentrated in the Federal Reserve Bank system is an unspeakable monstrosity that is self-empowered to create money panics, causing depressions and money shortages at will to suit its own greedy and nefarious purposes as Lincoln foresaw long ago.

A historic example of Lincoln's honest money system, based upon the integrity and productivity of the government's issuing it, occurred in the last years of the Civil War. President Lincoln needed money to conclude the war, and since the bankers wanted such absurd interest, he instead decided to ask Congress to issue interest-free United States notes (the greenbacks) to cover the amount that was needed, $450 million. The Congress did so under the power granted it by Article I of the Constitution. Every effort was made by the international bankers to attack this issue of funds, and the notes were derisively called Lincoln greenbacks. But to this day, there are still some in circulation and they are, in fact, the only lawful currency of the United States. There is much evidence that international bankers who feared interest-free currency may have ordered the assassination of Abraham Lincoln. By official count, these greenbacks have to date saved the United States $50 billion alone.

Were our president today to follow Lincoln's example, there would be no devaluation of the dollar, no financial crisis, and no more billions in interest to pay yearly to the holders of stock in the Federal Reserve corporation for the use of money that we print for them for the price of paper and ink. It is clear that the current president and the members of Congress, both House and Senate, are more concerned for the welfare of the international bankers who, in our opinion, pay them for their misdirected loyalty.

We ask the readers, where are the true leaders today who will champion the cause of moral right in monetary policy for all American citizens in the legislature? Are there truly no more principled "Honest Abes" to be found among us? Could it be you? Is it your congressperson or senator?

Andrew Jackson was perhaps the American president who best understood the banker mentality. He said:

If the American people understood the banking system, there would be revolution in the morning...If Congress has the right under the Constitution to issue paper money, it was given to them to be used by themselves, not to be delegated to individuals or corporations.

In 1836, Jackson explained why he refused to sign a renewal for the private Second Bank of the United States:

This organized Money Power would from its secret conclave have dictated the choice of your (American people) highest officers and compelled you to make peace or war, as best suited their own wishes.

In 1921, President Franklin Roosevelt wrote to Col. E.M. House:

> You and I both know that financial elements (banks) in the larger centers (cities) have owned the government since the days of Andrew Jackson.

Jackson once said to the bankers who approached him in the White House attempting to renew their corporate powers under a federal charter:

> Gentlemen, I have had men watching you for a long time and I am convinced that you have used the funds of the bank to speculate in the foodstuffs of the country. When you won, you divided the profits amongst you, and when you lost, you charged it to the bank. You tell me that if I take the deposits from the bank and annul its charter I shall ruin ten thousand families. That may be true, gentlemen, but that is your sin. Should I let you go on you will ruin fifty thousand families, and that would be my sin. You are a

den of vipers and thieves! I have determined to rout you out, and by the
Eternal God, I will rout you out!

The Congressional Record documents that Nicho-
las Biddle, head of the Second (central) Bank of the
United States, sought Jackson's support for a new
banking law that Jackson considered unfair. Jackson refused. Angered, Biddle threatened to "cause a financial
panic." Jackson told him, "You do, and I'll hang you to
the first tree I can find!" History records that Biddle
did not cause his money panic.

Jackson survived at least three assassination at-
tempts on his life, and although not proven, it seems
most likely to have been by those favoring and supporting the central banking concepts.

Dealing with the bankers in his farewell address,
Andrew Jackson, in the colorful language of the day,
said:

The immense capital and peculiar privi-
leges bestowed upon it (the Second
Bank of the United States) enabled it
to exercise despotic sway over the other banks in every part of the country.
From its superior strength it could seri-
ously injure, if not destroy the business
of any of them which might incur its

resentment; and it openly claimed for itself the power of regulating the currency throughout the United States. In other words, it asserted (and undoubtedly possessed) the power to make money plenty or scarce at its pleasure, at any time and in any quarter of the Union, by controlling the issues of other banks and permitting an expansion or compelling a general contraction of the circulating medium, according to its own will. The other banking institutions were sensible of its strength, and they soon became its obedient instruments, ready at all times to execute its mandates...

From Jackson's conclusion in his farewell speech:

In the hands of this formidable power, thus organized, was also placed unlimited dominion over the amount of the circulating medium, giving it the power to regulate the value of property and the fruits of labor in any quarter of the Union, and to bestow prosperity or bring ruin upon any city or section of the country as might best comport with its own interest or policy. Yet, if you had not conquered, the government would have passed from the hands of the many to the hands of the few, and this organized money power from its secret conclave would have dictated the choice of your highest officers and compelled you to make peace or war, as best suited their own wishes. The forms of government might for a time have remained, but its living spirit would have departed from it.

It is interesting to consider that President John F. Kennedy was assassinated only five months after he signed Executive Order # 11110, little known, but still in effect, which returned the federal government the power to issue constitutional currency itself without going through the Federal Reserve. Kennedy's order to issue silver certificates backed by silver bullion, silver, or silver dollars, brought nearly $4.3 billion in US notes into circulation, and could have prevented the national debt from reaching its current levels. We know that this could well have cut into the profits of the banking establishment. Could his assassination have been a warning to future politicians to toe the Fed line, or else? Why else has no sitting president utilized Executive Order # 11110, which has not even been rescinded, but just ignored?

Many Americans somehow still refuse to believe that bankers can start wars. Concerning World War I, in the Senate Document No. 346, 67th Congress, 4th Session, documented by Thomas Porter in *The Green Magicians*, the author concludes:

> We repeat, and respectfully submit, that in view of the foregoing facts, it is clearly established that Hungary did not cause and did not bring about the last world war (WWI). **The responsibility for the last world war rests solely upon the shoulders of international (Capital) financiers.** It is they upon whose head the blood of millions of dead and millions of dying rests.

See also Senate Document No. 40, 4th Congress, 1st Session, 8253 on the cause and planning of WWI.

In 1935, before World War II, bankers, intervened because they were alarmed that Germany, was rapidly recovering from the devastation of WWI and horrendous inflation by using government-issued debt-free money. Thomas Porter quotes from *The Word*, published in Glasgow, Scotland:

> …Marriner Eccles of the Federal Reserve Board and Montague Norman of the Bank of England agreed not later than 1935 on the joint policy of killing

Hitler's financial experiment (in debt-free money) by all methods, including war, if necessary.

Also in *The Green Magicians,* Porter quotes from *The Citadels of Chaos,* by Cornelius Carl Veith:

The big bankers were alarmed at the success of Germany's money just as their families were alarmed generations ago at the success of Lincoln's money. The very words of consternation uttered at Lincoln equally describe their chagrin at Hitler's progress, namely: "If that mischievous financial policy... should become indurated down to a fixture (become banking policy) then that government will furnish its own money without cost. It will pay off its own debts and be without debt. It will have all the money necessary to carry on its own commerce. It will become prosperous beyond precedent in the history of the civilized countries of the world...The brains and the wealth of all countries will go to North America. **That government must be destroyed or it will destroy every monarchy on the globe**...What might have been a laudable program on the part of Germany was thus the principle cause of World War II. The fight between rival monetary policies was inevitable.

While the list of the sins of the Money Power is long, one of the most despicable things it ever did was to build the Soviet Union from a sixth– or seventh-rate military power to a point where nuclear war was technically possible.

Let us not forget also that corporations affiliated with the Money Power also sold military material to the Soviet Union, which transferred it to North Vietnam, which then used it to kill the 58,000 plus soldiers who died there. The details can be reviewed in the speech that Dr. Anthony Sutton made to the 1972 Republican Convention. Dr. Sutton's speech listed the war material, and the names of the Soviet ships that delivered it to North Vietnam.

It is beyond the scope of this book to do anything more than briefly expound upon the financial causes of the various wars although there are numerous examples that could be provided. The in-depth interested reader will easily find ample documented occurrences that leave little doubt that self-interested money creators and controllers are the cause of wars.

AMERICAN FREE PRESS   October 2001

INJUSTICE CONTINUES: THE STATUS QUO

Gertrude M. Coogan reveals in *Money Creators* that, in reality, privilege governs the United States. President Herbert Hoover privately admitted that he knew that the monetary policies in force should be changed. When Hoover was asked why, as president, he did nothing to effect this change, he answered that **those in charge of the Federal Reserve would not allow him to act, or to even make his knowledge known to the public.**

Hoover's admission makes the point that if the president of the United States is not more powerful than the Fed, and he is not, that one fact alone (there are many others) is proof it should be abolished or at least placed under the US Treasury and controlled by Congress.

American citizens who do not understand the current financial reality in 2007 in the United States, as articulated in *Monetary Science Publications*, are, in kindness, not fully informed:

The banking industry ... becomes the socio-economic czar and the unelected sovereign to which the lawful debt emasculated governments, have perhaps, in ignorance, surrendered their sovereignty, be-

trayed their citizenry, their business and labor, and delivered themselves as slaves to the international deposits credits money dominance... The real financial powers of the world are in the hands of investment bankers (often called "international" or "merchant" bankers) who remain largely behind the scenes in their own unincorporated private banks. These form a system of international cooperation and dominance of nations—which is more private, more powerful, and more secretive than that of their agents in central banks.

Carroll Quigley, in *Tragedy and Hope: A History of the World in Our Time,* outlines the outstanding characteristics of the international bankers:

They remained different from ordinary bankers in distinctive ways: 1) They were cosmopolitan and international. (2) They were close to governments and were concerned with questions of government debts... (3) Their interests were almost exclusively in bonds and rarely in goods... (4) They were accordingly fanatical devotees of deflation... (5) They were always equally devoted to secrecy and the secret use of financial influence in political life. These bankers came to be called "international bankers" and more particularly, were known as "merchant bankers" in England, "private bankers" in France, and "investment bankers" in the United States. In all countries, they carried on various kinds of banking and exchange activities, but everywhere they were sharply distinguishable from other, more obvious kinds of banks, such as savings banks or commercial banks.

Although he is presented publicly in the nation's press as the head of the Fed, Ben Bernanke is, in a sense, just an errand boy for the owners of the international banks. Like his predecessor, Alan Greenspan, he is there only to do their bidding. Mr. Bernanke too is really in the service of the owners of the central banks, but is well compensated.

Our money system needs to be changed to benefit American citizens, and unless we change it soon, we face national bankruptcy.

This is not opinion. It is mathematics. The amount of money in circulation is now always far less than the amount of the national debt. The fact is, even if every

Federal Reserve note were called in, it would not even come close to being enough to pay off the debt to the bankers, which is now at over $9 trillion and is growing at the mind boggling approximate rate of $30 million an hour!

Mr. Ron Supinski of the Federal Reserve Bank of San Francisco admitted this information to researcher Dan Benham during a telephone interview in 2002, and it is documented on the Internet at d.benham@ worldnet.att.net. We currently owe some $9 trillion to the national debt, but there are roughly 650 billion Federal Reserve notes in circulation.

We are in this mess largely because our central banking industry has usurped our country's constitutional right that **Congress "…shall have the Power to Coin Money and regulate the Value thereof."** Most American citizens do not know that the banking industry, a few thousand private citizens, non-elected, now have more power than the president, the Congress, and the American people. It is highly significant that the Fed has **NEVER** been independently audited and still will not allow it.

A study by the Church of Scotland describes the central banking concept:

The essential truth remains that the banking system monetizes the credit of the community, that is, its real wealth, and lends this money to the community as interest-bearing debt …**the basis of the banking system is on this account fraudulent in the strict sense of the word**… the existing system of debt finance whereby practically all money comes into existence as interest-bearing debt is prejudicial to human well-being, a drag on the development and distribution of wealth, finds no justification in the nature of things, and perpetuates a wrong conception of the function of money in human society… **the credit of the community belongs to the community, and its transformation into community debt is morally wrong**.

This explanation, given by the Church of Scotland, is the present truth of our economic policy and represents the heart of the matter. It is the very reason the Constitution provided for the issue and the regulation of money by Congress for the public good, and not for private benefit. The wise Founding Fathers did this in the hope that it would prevent "love of money" from destroying the republic they had founded. **As things now are, the central banking system in place uses the credit of the nation, its real wealth, as the basis for**

money creation, and then lends the money to the nation as interest-bearing debt.

We can see that the subversion of Article I of the Constitution has brought on us the evil of the false worship of money. Our present banking system is based on a moral wrong and is the reason our country is in such a financial mess.

In a letter to the editor in *The American Free Press*, Anthony Snow wrote:

> Honest money is not made honest by specie. It is made honest by honesty. **Private money cannot ever be truly honest, even if it wishes to, because of the profit necessity**. Only national money controlled by national law can make money honest.

An intellectually honest banker, Sir Josiah Stamp, who was a president of the Bank of England, gave an informal talk to students at the University of Texas in 1920. The quote is documented in Appendix C, of *Money* by James Ewart:

> Banking was conceived in iniquity and born in sin. Bankers own the world. Take it away from them, but leave them with the power to create money and with the flick of a pen (or computer),

they will create enough money to buy it back again. Take this power away from bankers and all great fortunes like mine will disappear, and they ought to disappear, because this would then be a better and happier world to live in. **But if you want to continue to be slaves of bankers, and pay the cost of your own slavery, let them, instead of your government, continue to create money.**

Another rare banker with a change of heart, Mr. Robert Hemphill, a former credit manager of the Federal Reserve Bank of Atlanta, said:

We are completely dependent on the...banks. Someone has to borrow every dollar we have in circulation, cash or credit. If the banks create ample synthetic money, we are prosperous. If not, we starve. We are absolutely without a permanent money system. When one gets a complete grasp upon the picture, the tragic absurdity of our hopeless position is almost incredible ...but there it is. **It (the money problem) is the most important subject intelligent persons can investigate**

and reflect upon. It is so important that our present civilization may collapse unless it is widely understood and the defects remedied.

To remedy our defective money system means to take fraud out of the banking system. We can accomplish this by changing the law to place the Fed under the US Treasury.

Gertrude M. Coogan, in *Money Creators*, writes:

Had the money system which Lincoln demanded and which was provided for by the Constitution of the United States (the greenbacks) been established, no other country would have been able to maintain a dishonest money system for the simple reason that the people of other nations would have seen the great blessings flowing from it, and one nation after another would have cast off the ancient shackles of the private money manipulators.

We thank the *American Free Press* for this portion of a special reprint of a classic report by the late pastor Sheldon Emry, "Billions for the Bankers, Debts for the People":

Americans, living in what is called the richest nation on earth, seem always to be short of money. Wives are working in unprecedented numbers, husbands hope for overtime hours to earn more, or take part-time jobs evenings and weekends, children look for odd jobs for spending money, the family debt climbs higher, and psychologists say one of the biggest causes of family quarrels and breakups is "arguments over money." **Much of this trouble can be traced to our debt-money system**...

MONEY IS MAN'S ONLY "CREATION"

...Economists use the term "create" when speaking of the process by which money comes into existence. Now, creation means making something that did not exist before. Lumbermen make boards from trees, workers build houses from lumber, and factories manufacture automobiles from metal, glass, and other materials. But in all these they did not "create," they only changed existing materials into a more usable and, therefore, more valuable form. This is not so with money. Here, and here alone, mankind actually "creates" something out of nothing. A little piece of paper of little value is printed so that it is worth a piece of lumber. Its value has been "created" in the true sense of the word.

MONEY "CREATING" PROFITABLE

As is seen by the above, money is very cheap to make, and whoever does the "creating" of money in a nation can make a tremendous profit! Builders work hard to realize a profit of 5% above their cost to build a house.

Auto manufacturers sell their cars at around 1% to 2% above the cost of manufacture and it is considered good business. But money "manufacturers" have no limit on their profits, since a few cents will print a $1 bill or a $10,000 bill.

That profit is part of our story, but first let us consider another characteristic of the thing—money, the love of which is the root of all evil.

ADEQUATE MONEY SUPPLY NEEDED

An adequate supply of money is indispensable to civilized society. We could forego many other things, but without money, industry would grind to a halt, farms would become only self-sustaining units, surplus food would disappear, jobs requiring the work of more than one person or one family would remain undone, shipping and large movements of goods would cease, hungry people would plunder and kill to remain alive, and all government except family or tribe would cease to function.

An overstatement, you say? Not at all. Money is the blood of civilized society, the means of all commercial trade except simple barter. It is the measure

AMERICAN FREE PRESS October 2001

and the instrument by which one product is sold and another purchased. Remove the money or even reduce the supply below that which is necessary to carry on current levels of trade and the results are catastrophic. For an example, we need only look at America's Depression of the early 1930s.

THE BANKERS' DEPRESSION OF THE 1930s

In 1930 America did not lack industrial capacity, fertile farmland, and willing workers or industrious farming families. It had an extensive and highly efficient transportation in railroads, road networks, and inland and ocean waterways. Communications between regions and localities were the best in the world, utilizing telephone, teletype, and radio, and a well-operated government mail system. No war ravaged the cities or the countryside, no pestilence weakened the population, nor had famine stalked the land. The United States of America in 1930 lacked only one thing: an adequate supply of money to carry on trade and commerce.

In the early 1930s, bankers, the only source of new money and credit, deliberately refused loans to industries, stores, and farms. Payments on existing loans were required, however, and money rapidly disappeared from circulation. Goods were available to be purchased, jobs were waiting to be done, but the lack of money brought the nation to a standstill. By this simple ploy, America was put in a "depression," and the greedy bankers took possession of hundreds of thousands of farms, homes, and business properties. The people were told "times are hard" and "money is short." Not understanding the system, they were cruelly robbed of their earnings, their savings, and their property.

MONEY FOR PEACE? NO! MONEY FOR WAR? YES!

World War II ended the "depression." The same Bankers who, in the early '30s, had no loans for peace-time houses, food, and clothing, suddenly had unlimited billions to lend [at interest] for Army barracks, K-rations, and uniforms! A nation that in 1934, could not produce food for sale, suddenly could produce bombs to send free to Germany and Japan!

With the sudden increase in money, people were hired, farms sold their produce, factories went to two shifts, mines re-opened, and "The Great Depression" was over! Some politicians were blamed for it and others took credit for ending it. The truth is the lack of money (caused by the Bankers) brought the depression and adequate money ended it. The people of America were never told that simple truth and in this article we will endeavor to show how these same Bankers who control our money and credit have used their control to plunder America and place us in bondage.

We agree with Mr. Emry's views on the "creation" of money, but must acknowledge the noble "creations" of music, art, and literature, all also from the causal realm of ideas, made manifest in the physical world. Money indeed, is also a "creation" of humankind and is first founded in an idea. We can choose to make the idea of money work for us instead of against us.

The true story of the sources of the Great Depression, as well as other deliberately instituted money panics, and subsequent foreclosures and seizures of property, appears in detail in *The Federal Reserve Conspiracy*. It is telling that the information outlined in Eustace Mullins' book was at the time of its publication so damning in its exposé, the book was actually banned and burned in Europe, the very source of our current banking system. Surely this is an indication of how very badly the bankers did not want Americans to have access to the material in this excellent book.

According to Stephen Zarlenga, founder of The American Monetary Institute, Eustace Mullins's book is still generally banned from discussions in the economics departments of American universities. He points out that Mullins was a student of the late Ezra Pound, who had a deep awareness of monetary principles, understood the abstract nature of money and its importance to society. Pound himself directed his students to examine the monetary studies of Alexander Del Mar, a money historian of the early 1900s.

As a librarian at the Library of Congress, Eustace Mullins has great credentials. In the compiling and writing of *The Federal Reserve Conspiracy*, he also had intimate access to the Library's vast resources in professional personnel and friends as well as its catalogued information.

Money can be used to either free or enslave. Which do you think is happening today?

The following chart from the pamphlet *Modern Money Mechanics,* published by the Federal Reserve Bank of Chicago, illustrates how "fractional reserve" banking works:

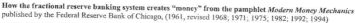

How the fractional reserve banking system creates "money" from the pamphlet *Modern Money Mechanics* published by the Federal Reserve Bank of Chicago, (1961, revised 1968; 1971; 1975; 1982; 1992; 1994)

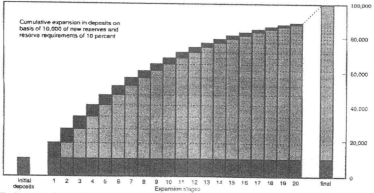

The Chart shows how an initial deposit of $10,000 gets magnified into $100,000 assuming a fractional reserve requirement of 10%. The first bank lends $9,000 keeping a 10% reserve. This gets spent and deposited into other banks which then loan out $8,100 keeping a 10% reserve. This gets spent and deposited into the banking system which then loans out $7,290 keeping a 10% reserve, etc, etc. Eventually $100,000 of checkbook "money" goes into circulation; $90,000 of it as bank loans, or debt, on which interest payments are required. An individual banker might not see it this way and might say he does not create money - he gets a "deposit."(of credit) and only loans out 90% if it! But system-wide, new money is being created. Fractional reserves constitute a special money creation privilege to the banking system. Its at the base of the undue concentration of wealth in America (this is a summary portrayal. The full process is more complex including different reserve requirements for different types of banks).

The "fractional reserve" banking system used by the Fed actually "creates" money from nothing by magnifying what they actually have by a factor of ten.

This means the banks are legally authorized by their own "creation" of the Federal Reserve Act to lend ten times the money they actually have on hand as interest-bearing credit. Only the bankers benefit from this arrangement. Everyone else who borrows the created money benefits only in terms of debt.

Peter Cook, in *Modern Money Mechanics: Capitalism, Socialism for Bankers,* says:

The banking industry is the only industry in the United States that gets its cash flow funds at no cost, from the mother capital banks, the Federal Reserve Banks. The Federal Reserve Banks are not part of the United States Government, but are 12 private corporations, incorporated May 18, 1914. The Federal Reserve Banks distribute the cash currency bills from the Treasury's Printing and Engraving Bureau for the paper, ink, and printing-labor cost, today estimated at about fourteen cents per bill of any imprinted value. The Federal Reserve Banks distribute the cash flow currency amongst the member banks in exchange for their so-called "reserve accounts credits," which reserve accounts are indirectly provided to the commercial banks at no cost by the mother banks—The Federal Reserve Banks.

No other business or industry in the United States, not even the government, ever gets a gift of free cash flow funds. Putting it in the simplest terms, the US Congress, in its generosity to the banking industry, perhaps in educated ignorance, contributes to the success of the bankers' selfish version of capitalism by tacitly running deficits—borrowing back its own printed currency at full imprinted face value—at taxpayer expense. To add insult to injury, using perhaps ultimate insider information, banks invest in the economy on their own account, creating unfair competition for the other businesses in America. **It would be almost impossible to find a more unfair system for American citizens.**

One of the best summaries of our dangerous central banking system is a monograph by Dr. Edwin Vieira Jr., published by the National Alliance for Constitutional Money Inc., titled *The Federal Reserve Banking System: Fatal Parasite on the American Body Politic.* In it, Vieira says:

> ...today's scheme of Federal-Reserve-System fiat currency and fractional-reserve banking is **plainly unconstitutional, inherently fraudulent**, economically unworkable in the long run, and subversive of America's political traditions of individual liberty and private property.

It is hard to imagine a situation that is more absurd or more morally wrong. The most powerful (private) agency in America, the Fed controls the lives of every American, every day!

The Federal Reserve Bank, domiciled in the United States and earning its income and profits from the economic efforts of the American people, is not accountable either to the government, or to the people whom it falsely claims to serve. Thanks to the greedy bankers, **our government is not a true democracy, but is really a plutocracy.**

Webster's dictionary defines a plutocracy as "government by the wealthy" or "a group of wealthy people who control or influence a government." This is exactly the situation we now have. Our America of "We, the People", is no longer a democratic republic envisioned by the Founding Fathers, but is now close to becoming a totalitarian state run by fascists.

The "Achilles' heel" of the current banking system is that it is morally wrong, and many of America's ills stem directly from it. It is beyond absurd, unconscionable, and criminal that our elected representatives of our great nation would willingly choose for it to go into such massive debt unnecessarily to a few private interests. This would happen only if they were (1) ignorant of sound and moral monetary principles, (2) ignorant of the history of past fallen civilizations due to the same sort of money policies now in existence, or (3) they greatly benefit from its continued operation through bribes and payoffs by banking lobbyists. Most likely, it is a combination of all three.

The early American colonies successfully used debt-free money. In *The Green Magicians*, Thomas Porter, documents that on a visit to England, Benjamin Franklin was asked how he accounted for the prosperous condition of the Colonies. Franklin replied:

It is because in the Colonies we issue our own paper money. We call it Colonial Script and we issue enough to move all goods freely from the producers to the consumers; and as we create our money, we control the purchasing power of money and have no interest to pay.

It was only at the end of the revolution, when England, as a war measure, flooded the colonies with counterfeit money, that the value of this money was destroyed.

Benjamin Franklin explained that the Rothschild Bank of England learned of the prosperous condition of the American Colonies, and saw the opportunity to exploit them. The Rothschild Bank caused a law to be passed by the English Parliament that no English colony could issue its own money, but was required to use English money. Franklin stated that in one year from that date the streets of the colonies were filled with the unemployed, because where England exchanged with them, she gave them only half as many units in borrowed money from the Rothschilds as they had in colonial script. In other words, their circulating medium was reduced 50%, and everyone became unemployed!

Abraham Lincoln paid much of the cost of the Civil War with government-issued debt-free money, the greenbacks. From 1935 to 1945, Germany used government-issued debt-free money to build a modern industrial nation. **Lincoln understood sound monetary principles and gave the best advice on money.** He said:

> The government should create, issue, and circulate all the currency and credit needed to satisfy the spending power of the government and the buying power of consumers. The privilege of creating and issuing money is not only the supreme prerogative of government, but is the government's greatest opportunity. **Money will cease to be the master and become the servant of the people. Democracy will rise superior to the money power.**

An example of the diametrically opposed view given by Lincoln is now our economic reality. David Rockefeller said in Baden, Germany, in 1991:

> The super-national sovereignty of an intellectual elite and world bankers is surely preferable to the national auto determination practiced in past centuries.

Mr. Rockefeller certainly does not speak for these writers, and respectfully, we do not think he speaks for most Americans. Such arrogance boggles the mind.

The national media won't tell the truth about money. Years ago, in 1914 at the New York Press Club, Mr. John Swinton, who at the time was the chief editor of the *New York Times* and one of the best-known newspapermen, was asked for a toast at the annual dinner of the American Press Association. Thomas Porter in *The Green Magicians* and James Ewart, in *Money*, document the toast given:

> There is no such thing as an independent press in America, if we except that of little country towns. You know this and I know it. Not a man among you dares to utter an honest opinion. Were you to utter it, you know beforehand that

it would never appear in print. I am paid weekly for keeping my honest opinion out of the paper. Others of you are paid similar salaries for similar things, and any of you who would be so foolish as to write honest opinions would be out on the streets looking for another job. If I allowed my honest opinions to appear in one issue of the paper, before twenty-four hours my occupation would be gone. It is the duty of a New York journalist to lie, distort, to revile, to toady (fawn) at the feet of Mammon, and to sell his country, and his race for his daily bread, or what it amounts to the same thing, his salary. **We are the tools and vassals of the rich behind the scenes**. We are the marionettes. These men pull the strings, and we dance. Our time, our talents, our lives, our capacities are all the property of these men – We are intellectual prostitutes.

While there are good people in both the Democratic and Republican political parties, both are overly influenced by the money men who are really in control and who will not tell the truth about money. The presidents who have been elected from either of our political parties will not tell the truth about money. Due to our misguided monetary policy, they also, in truth are ruled and controlled by the investment bankers who determine who will populate the boards of the Federal Reserve, and who tell the presidents whom to appoint to these board positions.

From *Modern Money Mechanics:*

...money can and does buy wealth, security, luxury, power kings, rulers, dictators, congressmen, senators, presidents, bishops, preachers, teachers, union leaders, police, crime, assassinations, etc...in other words, **in money resides power, a power greater than law and ballot**.

From *Media By-Pass Magazine:*

America, Wake up! We have been conned with the big lie that we are free people, when the fact is we have become a nation of debt shackled, news controlled tax slaves of a few privileged bankers who control most all legislation, commerce, and " national news" in our country. We Americans

cannot get free from this insidious entrapment unless a majority awakens to this truth! Every American should be made aware of how they are being taken for uninformed fools to be robbed! By uniting, we 280,000,000 (now over 300,000,000) Americans can end this money swindle and its impoverishing income tax that is slowly but surely destroying all of us. We can stop allowing the money supply owners "national news" to guide our thoughts, actions, and votes. We must stop voting for career politicians. They are the ones who allow the privately owned Federal Reserve Banks to "steal" our nation's money supply and then lend it back to us as an illegal debt owed to them. We must stop electing anyone to Congress or the presidency who refuses to pledge to all of us that he/she will work to furnish our nation with a money supply that is spent, not loaned into circulation; free of debt and interest, which will end the enslaving and impoverishing income tax.

A friend of the monetary reform movement in south Mississippi, Mr. Steve Edson, CDR US Navy (ret.), wrote an excellent summary of our predicament in a letter to the editor, the Sun Herald, which was published on the Opinion—Editorial Page, May 15, 2003, under the caption **"Too few understand America's money system"**:

James Lester's letter of May 3 (2003) ("Debt-free money would create new problems") which was critical of Frank Wallace's letter of April 29 ("Government should have a fourth branch: Money"), exhibits a lack of understanding of out monetary system, an all-too common failing on our country. Consider:

The Fed is *not* a government entity; it is a private bank owned by the London/New York/European Merchant Banks.

Government issue of debt-free dollars is inflationary, but the issue of dollars by the Fed is equally inflationary. The trick is: *We pay interest* on the dollars the Fed creates out of thin air and 'lends' to the *treasury*. This increases the national debt and the bankers *love it*!

For 125 years the above-mentioned bankers tried to establish a central bank in the United States. Andrew Jackson stymied them; Lincoln defied them with his debt-free greenbacks; but they finally broke through in 1913 when they succeeded in passing the Federal Reserve Act. Despite senatorial opposition, the Act was passed by a small quorum of conspiratorial "banking-backed" senators taking advantage of the fact that almost all the senators were absent during Christmas recess.

John Maynard Keyes' deleterious effect on international finance via his "General Theory of Employment, Interest, and Money" upset the natural laws of finance and economic equilibrium. I'd suggest that Lester read *On the Horns of the Beast*, which I published, and watch the video, *The Money Masters*, which I produced. Both call for abolition of the Fed and return of the money power to Congress where it belongs. This could be

done by printing the money and paying off the national debt…

STEVE EDSON
Gautier, MS

In the *American Money Scene,* a quarterly bulletin
of the American Monetary Institute, founder and director Stephen Zarlenga writes:

At one point [in history], metals were
mistakenly enthroned as a substitute for real money. Today, interest-
bearing credit, loaned by private banks
is being brazenly substituted for money.
This automatically transfers power and
wealth to bankers and financiers. But
there is nothing in their training, expe-
rience, and philosophy or souls, that
qualifies them for such control over
mankind, and they have misdirected society for centuries. With modern weapons this misdirection risks the annihila-
tion of the species.

Stephen Zarlenga's book *The Lost Science of Money:
The mythology of Money—The Story of Power* is a mas-
terly thesis utilizing over 800 source materials, and outlines both what has gone wrong and also how to restore

sanity and morality to monetary policy. See www.monetary.org. From the promotional text of the book:

Unheard of wealth concentrates into very few, largely undeserving hands. Americans work harder and produce more than ever but increasingly fall into debt and bankruptcy while corruption rules and predators plunder society by merely shuffling papers. [Now] Less than 1% of the population owns about 50% of the wealth, and receives over 70% of the income! *The Lost Science of Money* shows how a false concept of money allowed it to happen, and tells how to reverse it. Information provided in this book exposes the mythology created to protect those who are embezzling from society, under cover of a deceptive ideology of money. This group has immorally used economic theory as a tool of class war for the past three hundred years, while screaming accusations of "class warfare" against those who question their power! ...An entire generation has been led astray into market worship and other forms of religious fundamentalism. **A dysfunction-**

al media focuses on the elections and sex habits of politicians while the real outcomes in society are determined behind the scenes by the structure of our nation's money system. This problem goes much deeper than accounting and stock fraud, and even beyond the graduate schools of business that inculcate such criminal behavior. **The deeper causes lie deeper in the structurally corrupt core of our banking system and our schools of economics. It arises from the falsehoods they have spread on the nature of money, allowing their patrons to control the money power, and in turn, to dominate our society.**

Zarlenga quotes the late Congressman Wright Patman, chairman of the House Committee on Banking and Currency for over sixteen years, as saying:

I have never yet had anyone who could, through the use of logic and reason, justify the federal government borrowing the use of its own money...I believe the time will come in this country when people will de-

mand that this be changed. I believe the time will come in this country when they will actually blame you and me and everyone else connected with the Congress for sitting idly by and permitting such an idiotic system to continue.

In a speech to the US House of Representatives on April 3, 1964, Congressman Patman said:

The fact is an independent Federal Reserve means something that is not in the framework of our constitutional system, which says that Congress will make the laws and the President will execute them. Those who desire a dictatorship on money matters by a "banker's club," away from the Congress and the President, are in effect advocating a form of government alien to our own.

Later Congressman Patman said:

In the United States we have, in effect, two governments…We have the duly constituted Government…Then **we have an independent, uncontrolled and uncoordinated government in**

the Federal Reserve System, operating the money powers which are reserved to Congress by the Constitution.

Marriner Eccles, a governor of the Federal Reserve Board, stated before Congress:

Debt is the basis for the creation of money.

From his testimony before the House Banking and Currency Committee, September 30, 1941:

Congressman Patman: Mr. Eccles, how did you get the money to buy those $2 billion of government securities?

Eccles: We created it.

Patman: Out of what?

Eccles: Out of the right to issue credit money.

During the time the international financial conspirators were flexing their financial muscles after the Great Depression, one US senator, Louis T. McFadden, who was for twenty-two years the chairman of the US House Banking and Currency Commission, said while addressing the House on June 10, 1932 (from 75 *Congressional Record* 12595-12603):

We have in this country one of the most corrupt institutions the world has ever known. I refer to the Federal Reserve Board and the Federal Reserve Banks, hereinafter called the Fed. Some people think the Federal Reserve Banks are US government institutions. **They are not government institutions. They are private monopolies which prey upon the people of the United States for the benefit of themselves and their foreign and domestic swindlers; rich and predatory moneylenders.**

The following facts are given by the American Monetary Institute of Valatie, New York and make clear that the **Fed is definitely not part of the US government:**

This information is available at www.monetary.org/federalreserveprivate.htm

1) The Federal Reserve System consists of 12 regional Federal Reserve banks, with boards of directors, under an umbrella direction of the seven members of the Federal Reserve Board in Washington, which has the power to determine major aspects

of banking activity, such as setting interest rates, and the reserve and other operational requirements. There are no shares of the Washington Fed Board organization; the only "ownership" of the Fed is in shares of each of the 12 regional banks. They are entirely owned by the private member banks in their respective districts, according to a formula on member bank size. The ownership is highly restricted in that such ownership is mandatory; the shares can't be sold; and they pay a guaranteed 6% annual dividend.

2) **The Fed is not organized within the Executive, Legislative, or Judicial branches of our government.**

3) **Who pays the Fed's bills and determines its budget? Not any part of our government**. The Fed gets its funding from its own specially privileged operations. The Fed board determines Fed budgets.

4) **Who monitors and oversees Fed activities? Again, the Fed itself**. While some important elements of proper auditing have taken place, there

has not yet been a comprehensive independent audit, by the Government Accountability Office as proposed in a recent letter from Mr. Ralph Nader to new Fed Chairman Ben Bernanke, calling for greater monetary transparency.

5) **Federal Reserve employees are not part of the US Civil Service System** and are not covered by government employees' health insurance or pension programs. Who does the hiring and firing? Except for the highly publicized Chairman and seven members of the Washington board, this is in private, unelected hands. The ambiguity surrounding the Fed arises because the US president appoints the Fed chairman to four-year terms, and the seven-member board to 14-year terms. Also, the Fed is supposed to implement government fiscal policy, but has not really done so.

6) **Federal Reserve banks are not listed as government organizations by the telephones, a small but telling fact**.

Zarlenga outlines several structural problems that arise from this private control:

> The system tends to be run to benefit those in control rather than the whole society. This concentrates wealth into fewer and fewer hands. The interest received by the banking system for money creation flows into their hands. **The control over where the money goes determines the direction of society moves in. Privately controlled money tends to go into speculation to make a quick buck. Infrastructure, health, and education get ignored and shortchanged...Most Americans think our money is issued and controlled by our government. They are surprised to learn that most of our money is created when people and businesses have to borrow from banks, since this is the main way that money now enters the system.** The banks make loans by crediting the borrowers' accounts. This is "fiat" money, or "purchasing media," created out of thin air, thanks to a special legal privilege granted to them called "fractional

reserve" banking. They write a computer credit in the account of those whose needs have driven them to the banking system to borrow money.

More background information from Stephen Zarlenga's American Monetary Institute:

1) **The actual history of government control over money shows a far superior record to private control.** There is a mythology—a reigning error—that government issued money has been irresponsible, and inflationary. But this is a result of decades, even centuries of relentless propaganda and is contradicted by the historical facts. The Continental Currency is attacked, without discussion that while our government authorized $200 million and issued exactly $200 million, the British successfully counterfeited untold billions. They did the same for the French Assignats and the details became public when the counterfeiters sued each other in the English courts. The American Greenbacks are smeared

as worthless inflation money when in fact our government authorized $450 million and printed exactly $450 million; and every Greenback eventually exchanged one for one with gold coinage—but very few people bothered to exchange them! The German hyperinflation is cited by the private money gang without pointing out that the German Reichsbank was privately owned and controlled, or that the hyperinflation began the month that all government influence over the Reichsbank was removed on the insistence of the allied occupiers. These and other cases are described in *The Lost Science of Money*.

2) The specter of inflation will be raised against any proposal that our government fulfill its responsibility to provide the nation's currency. Again, this is a knee-jerk reaction resulting from the same propaganda. The reason that inflation is avoided is that real wealth is created with the money spent into circulation on infrastructure, education, and health care. It results in the provision

of real goods and vital services and the existence of these serves to control inflation. **It is mainly expenditures for warfare that are inflationary, because not only is the money not directed to creating values for life, it actually destroys those values, while increasing the money supply.** That will always be inflationary.

3) It will be argued that the banks must have the money privilege in order to survive, and removing it will destroy banking. That is absurd. The Savings and Loan industry operated for many decades on principles that our Monetary Act advocates. **We are not out to destroy banking. It is a necessary part of modern society. However, we see the folly of making bankers the rulers of the universe.** There is nothing in their background, or training, or philosophy for that. Look at the mess that [banker control] has created all around the world.

4) This comprehensive American Monetary Act has its best chance for passage in the next financial crisis

our unethical banking system is in the process of creating. Because so much power exists in control of our money system, it is not possible to predict when just when, but the warning signs have been visible for years. **Our strategy is to educate as many citizens and lawmakers as we can on the monetary problem and its solution,** and to have The American Monetary Act ready so that when the next crisis hits (or the next one), there is a chance for passage.

5) **Lawmakers at the national level must be made to understand how this problem is within their power to solve.** At the state and local levels, lawmakers must be made aware how solving this problem nationally opens the way for real world solutions of most of the 'insoluble' local problems they face. Therefore, **in conjunction with the national approach, a state focused campaign needs to be organized**. None of this will be easy, but take heart when you consider that what we are proposing would be immensely beneficial to 99.5% of the population.

> Even those presently gaining unearned riches from the present faulty system would benefit from the improved quality and security of life in general.

Real proof that government issued debt-free money will work and function comes from the bankers themselves: A quotation in the *London Times* shortly after the Civil War announced:

If that mischievous financial policy, which had its origin in the North American Republic during the late war in that country, should become indurate down to a fixture (become banking practice), then that government will furnish its own money without cost. It will pay off its debts and become without a debt. It will have all the money necessary to carry on its commerce. It will become prosperous beyond precedent in the history of the civilized governments of the world. And the wealth of all countries will go to North America. That government must be destroyed or it will destroy every monarchy on the globe.

Banking industry claims that debt-free money will not work or function, choose to ignore the historical record and are unworthy of the serious consideration by responsible people.

One of the best books on money is *Debt Virus* by Dr. Jacques Jaikaran, a surgeon who was invited to join the board of directors of a bank in Temple, Texas. Because of the banking errors and irregularities that he found, Dr. Jaikaran conducted a seven-year study of our money system. *Debt Virus* is the result of his research and is short, comprehensive, and superb.

In *Debt Virus*, Dr. Jacques Jaikaran explains:

> Since 1822, the English Island of Guernsey, has run no government debt, because, the Guernsey States Government prints its own currency, instead of borrowing bank-printed currency at a high interest cost, as does the United States Government.

Debt Virus describes in detail how the Island of Guernsey has used debt-free state money since 1822. Income taxes there are about 9%, there is no national debt, no unemployment, average income is around $40,000 yearly, the value of an average house is about $140,000. Evidently, the people of the Island of Guernsey know something about money that we do not.

The following, courtesy of Steve Edson, CDR US Navy (ret.), is a photo replica of the front and reverse sides of real debt-free money being used today, THE STATES OF GUERNSEY One-Pound Note.

The introduction to *Debt Virus* offers:

Envision a world without poverty or economic oppression, a place where humankind can attain its potential

amidst the weightlessness of true freedom. Imagine the United States, and
the rest of the world, without hunger or
homelessness, where educated societies enjoy the fruits of their labor. In such
a society, it wouldn't be necessary to
hand over your hard-earned dollars to
the government to pay ever increasing
taxes. Could you learn to live in a place
where budgets were balanced, homes
were affordable, and you kept all the
money you earned? *Debt Virus* is an in-
triguing book that questions the traditional role of money in our economy. It
critically examines the current money-
creation process as the source of in-
stability in the United States and global
economies. Debt-ridden money, laced
with interest rate premiums, according to the author, is a deadly virus that
destroys the economic foundations of
society in that total debt repayment is
mathematically impossible. The debt
virus is no respecter of governments,
institutions, or individuals as it takes
its toll on savings, investment, employment, income, growth, and stability. Inflation, recession, and economic

depression are inevitable in an all-debt monetary system, and conventional explanations of these economic phenomena are grossly inadequate...

From *Weekly World News*, March 9, 1996, with the caption "Tiny English Island is the Happiest Place On Earth!":

An astonishing 97% of Guernsey's 55,000 residents say they are happy—compared to just 33% of people in the United States, according to a Gallup poll.

The Credit-Money Blue Book, written by Peter Cook and published by Monetary Science Publishing, provides details about the Guernsey States:

The government runs no deficits and has no fear of getting in governmental debt, because, the Guernsey States Government prints its own currency, instead of borrowing bank-printed currency at a high interest cost, estimated at about $300 billion in 1994. The island has low taxes, high incomes, little pollution, and NO political parties!

How it is done and how it can be done is explained in: *The Guernsey Experiment* by Olive and Jan Grubiak, *Debt Virus* by Dr. Jaikaran, and *The Credit-Money Blue Book* by Peter Cook.

Shortly after the Civil War, the European bankers started planning and plotting to insinuate their greedy schemes into American politics to be able to gradually take complete control of the country through little-understood financial schemes and methods. To say they succeeded would be a vast understatement.

Readers might be surprised to know that during the Civil War (between the North and South) in this country, two Rothschild banks—one in London and the other in Paris—funded the war. According to the research of Jim Marrs in *Rule by Secrecy*, the Rothschild brothers supplied more money to the North, which, of course, prevailed in the (some say planned) conflict.

When President Woodrow Wilson was about to sign the bill creating the Fed, Minnesota Congressman Charles A. Lindbergh (father of the famous flier), said, "**When the president signs this bill, the invisible government will be legalized.** Congressman Lindberg also said in *Lindberg on the Federal Reserve*:

> I was a member of the banking committee in the House when the Federal Reserve Act was passed. I was the only

member of the committee to strenuously oppose the act and its subsequent use as a whip over the people. The Federal Reserve ... producing an expansion of credit and a rising stock market ... it can check prosperity in mid-career ... it can cause the pendulum of rising and falling markets ... and it will possess the inside information ... of advance knowledge of the coming changes, either up or down ... This is the strangest, most dangerous advantage ever placed in the hands of a special privilege class by any government that ever existed. **This system is private, conducted for the sole purpose of obtaining the greatest possible profits from the use of other people's money ... it is inconsistent with free government** ... to subject to the domination of big banks which have been granted the exclusive privilege to control our finances ... The banks have been granted the power to create panics when they please ... The Money Trust to inflate and deflate the country at their pleasure ... They also know in advance where to create panics to their advantage. They also know when to stop a panic. Inflation and deflation work equally well for them.

In commenting on the financial turmoil of the 1920s, Lindbergh said:

Under the Federal Reserve Act, panics are scientifically created; the present panic is the first scientifically created one, worked out as we figure a mathematical solution.

In 1916, commenting on his part in the Fed creation, President Woodrow Wilson, whose signature in 1913 ratified the Federal Reserve Act, said, **"I am a most unhappy man. Unwittingly, I have ruined my country."** In his book *The Federal Reserve Hoax: The Age of Deception*, Wickliffe B. Vennard Sr. quotes Wilson:

A great industrial nation is controlled by its system of credit. Our system of credit is concentrated. The growth of the Nation and all of our activities are concentrated in the hands of a few men. We are one of the worst ruled, one of the most completely controlled and dominated governments on earth—no longer a government of free opinion, no longer a government by conviction and vote of the majority, but a government by the opinion and duress of small groups of dominant men.

Wickliffe Vennard had this to say about President Wilson:

Wilson set the sails on our Ship of State, and his followers pursued the same course—into oblivion. Wilson and Roosevelt were in possession of all knowledge and all of their faculties when they lied us into World War I and World War II. They willingly and wittingly brought death to millions in order to crown themselves "king of the world" under the League of Nations and United Nations, respectively.

President Wilson reportedly stated to friends that he had been "deceived," and that he had "betrayed" his country. Wilson was referring to the Federal Reserve Act passed during his presidency.

US Senator Carter Glass, sponsor of the Federal Reserve Act, said in 1938:

I had never thought **the Federal Bank System would prove such a failure.**

The country is in a state of irretrievable bankruptcy.

The only thing that can correct this situation is honest open dialogue, which is now a sacrosanct non-subject in the media, education, politics, and religion. The power that the bankers have usurped from we, the people have allowed them to gain ownership, and thus nearly complete control of most of the "news" we receive daily, and also how our children are educated. We need to strip the banks of their power to create money as debt and adopt a method of money creation whereby the US Treasury creates our money for the efficient facilitation of commerce in proper proportion as and when needed, as given and recommended by the Founding Fathers.

Dr. Jaikaran advises us in *Debt Virus*:

When ancient Egypt fell, only 4% of the population held all the wealth. When the Babylonian civilization collapsed, only 3% of the people owned all the wealth. When ancient Persia was destroyed, 2% of the people owned all the wealth. When ancient Greece sank into ruin, only 0.5% of the people held all the wealth. When the Roman Empire collapsed into ruin, only about two thousand people owned all the wealth in the known civilized world, and this debacle ushered in the period known as the Dark Ages.

In 2008, this same set of dire circumstances in America exists with 1% of the people owning over 50% of the wealth, yet we continue to repeat the same mistake that contributed and led to the collapse of these ancient civilizations, and we do it with an alarming air of ignorance and inaction! What awful legacy are we leaving to our children and grandchildren?

In *Money Reformist*, Mel Jones quotes David Rockefeller, internationalist and multibillionaire, member of the Bilderbergers, the Council on Foreign Relations, Trilateral Commission founder, and the godfather of the New World Order as he voiced his praise of the US media for keeping their oath not to divulge their "globalist" and elitist plans to the public. Speaking to his fellow conspirators at a Bilderberger (another New World Order organization) meeting in Baden, Germany, in June 1991, Rockefeller said:

We are grateful to the *Washington Post*, the *New York Times*, *Time Magazine*, and other publications whose directors have attended our meetings and respected their promise of discretion for almost forty years ... It would have been impossible for us to develop **our plan for the world** if we had been subject to the bright lights of publicity during those years. But, the world is now more sophisticated and prepared to march towards a world government. **The super-national sovereignty of an intellectual elite and world bankers is surely preferable to the national auto-determination in past centuries.**

In our opinion, this infuriating statement borders on treason. So does the next.

John D. Rockefeller, one of the early activists on the educational front, bragged about his plans for education in his *Occasional Letter No. 1,* issued by the Rockefeller Educational Board:

In our dreams **we have limitless resources and the people yield themselves with perfect docility to our molding hands**. The present educational conventions fade from our minds, and unhampered by tradition, **we will work our own good upon a grateful and unresponsive rural folk**. We shall not try to make these people

or any of their children into philosophers or men of learning, or of science. We have not to raise up from
among them authors, editors, poets,
or men of letters. We shall not search
for embryo great artists, musicians,
nor lawyers, doctors, preachers, politicians, statesmen of whom we now
have ample supply ... so we will organize our children into a little community and teach them to do in a perfect way the things their fathers and
mothers are doing in an imperfect
way, in the homes, in the shop, and
on the farm.

This is a powerful clue to precisely what has become wrong with our educational system, apparently
by design. **Our children have long been taught what
to think, not how to think.**

As society has "progressed" into the modern digital
era, we can see that paper and coin money is now on
its way out, to be replaced with electronic debit "smart"
card systems using cashless transactions. Our government tells us that we will all benefit by protection from
fraud and ease of use, but this is just a clever attack on
our civil liberties. This is an insidious and ultimate way
for governments to control how we spend our money.

In *Secrets of the Freemasons*, Michael Bradley quotes Mr. Richard Poynder, chairman of the Smart Card Club, which encourages the use of electronic money, as saying:

Special software could actually prevent recipients of social security benefits from squandering their money on "banned products and services such as alcohol or gambling." We could ensure that they don't spend money on the 'wrong' things... A young man trying to spend his dole money in a bar would find his card refused by the central computer.

"Gradualism" combined with technology have made the predictions of author George Orwell, in his novel *1984*, a fast- approaching nightmare reality for all modern societies.

Another powerful clue to the power and influence of the bankers (and insurance companies) can be found by simple observation in any large metropolitan area or city. Take note of what buildings are the largest, most expensive, and dominate the landscape. This is most easily done by those with the power to create money at will.

Left unchecked, the bankers will in time dominate everything and everyone. Their unbridled power combined with the implements of modern technology, such as Radio Frequency Identifier Chips (RFIDS), the satellite Global Positioning System, millions of surveillance cameras, implantable microchips, smart ID cards, and a cashless society combined with the latest "Star Wars" types of remotely controlled systems of exotic microwave and infrared weapons will ensure there soon will be no escape from complete domination and exploitation.

It is the authors' fervent hope and prayer that we American citizens will arise from our slumbering ignorance and reclaim the political power that has been ours all along. We, the people can change it if we will. **We have the real power if we will but take it.**

A co-author of this treatise on money and truth, Frank Wallace, wrote *There Is a Way*, self-published, in 1957, which offered ways to improve race relations between the blacks and whites in the South. Frank wrote in *There Is a Way*:

Laws are grounded in morals, and what is morally wrong cannot make a good law.

This quote certainly applies to the Federal Reserve Act and its supporting companion, the Income Tax Act, both still dramatically affecting us all today.

INJUSTICE ENDS: RESTORING
MONETARY POWER TO AMERICANS

The good news is the last chapters of The *Lost Science of Money* by Stephen Zarlenga details a cure for our monetary ills by presenting **The Monetary Reform Act** to be presented to the legislature for consideration as a bill. The concepts are based on Aristotelian monetary concepts in existence since at least the 4th century BC. and were employed successfully in a variety of monetary systems since then, from democratic Athens to republican Rome. It is interesting to note that both of these advanced (for their time) societies fell into ruin after private money systems that usurped the sound money practices advocated by Aristotle were gradually implemented.

Zarlenga's exhaustive research proves beyond any doubt that **the control of money should shift away from private control toward governmental control**. It should move from commodity money notions, and away from fractional reserve banking—monetizing private credits and lending them into circulation as interest. He says:

We should move toward money issued interest free by government and spent into circulation for the common good.

The American Monetary Institute has a wonderful Internet web site, with the important educational information that outlines the way out of our collective financial mess by enacting the Monetary Reform Act through Congress. See www.monetary.org. Under this plan, our nation could be restored to greatness by issuing interest-free money for education, health care, infrastructure projects and repairs, and disaster relief. This would automatically create jobs and boost the economy in numerous positive ways.

We desperately need a new independent political party to tackle the supremely important matter of monetary reform.

A monetary reform party could make a good case against "free trade," the loss of our manufacturing base, and the fast shrinkage of our middle class. It could provide a political home for those who feel that the current "business is everything" attitude is not best for our country. **This party would understand that our money and tax system and its enforcers, the Federal Reserve Bank and the Internal Revenue Service, are a national disgrace.** It would also know that the United Nations in its current form is just an irresponsible debating society. The UN is weak because its member nations are nations in name only due to the fact that they also are now controlled by the same international banking interests. The new party could finally capture

The White House by supporting traditional and constitutional American values as a more humane contrast to the money-driven forces that now move world events by financing their money-driven wars.

The money manipulators in their greedy profit seeking have tragically caused the killing of countless veterans and innocents alike, and have broken the bodies of thousands. We believe that millions of responsible and decent Americans would be attracted to a new political party which dedicates itself to the cause of moral sanity in monetary reform.

Monetary Reform Talking Points to use in discussions with legislators, either sitting or potential and with the media:

1) **Monetary reform is not about economics** or any "explanation" (excuse) anyone may offer. **It IS about a fundamental and basic moral issue of what is right and wrong at our core as a sovereign nation.** We only raise the issue as thinking free citizens and ask the moral question: **Who should have the right to create, own and operate any monetary system?** Should it be a few private banking interests or the citizenry at large? More to the point and most importantly, who should directly benefit from the profits

generated from interest payments of any monetary system adopted? A conscience that is based on truth and morality will conclude that **the only correct answer dictates that all American citizens should benefit, not the private bankers**.

2) Arguably, **this is the ONLY meaningful issue of our times, as it exposes the root of all current problems in the United States, and the world by extension, and is our best and only true way to obtain hope and meaning for all American citizens, whether poor, average, or affluent**. We can continue to allow the bankers to service our money, but make them pay their own way like the rest of us. Why should the bankers alone have this fundamental right? Let us restore the balance to a more level playing field and elect an accountable congress of "We, the People" to create and manage the money. Any other action or issue, before addressing the issue of monetary reform, however well meaning or intentioned, is analogous to putting a Band-Aid on the cancer of our body politic and merely delays any possible positive outcome.

3) Reform of the monetary issue represents the greatest opportunity in a hundred years or more for members of a Monetary Reform Party to be real heroes of the American people by realigning with moral principle.

Consider that **three viewpoint versions of history exist:**

There is the view of **the victors,** published with ego bias by the media owners, presented in the "mainstream" press and television. This is what the controllers allow us to read.

There is the view of **the vanquished,** which is almost never published as written, and is usually and purposely obliterated over time. A prime example is the Egyptian Nag Hammadi texts, and the Dead Sea Scrolls, from Qumran discovered in 1945 and 1947, respectively. Thankfully, both precious collections survived so that scholars can make comparisons with the current versions in the New Testament and the King James Bible, and note the alterations made by folks who were the victors. Note also that it took over fifty years for the world to view them after their discovery.

Finally, there is the view of real history (**His Story**). Every thought, word, and deed is recorded in the skein of time and space on what is variously called the

Akashic records, The Quantum Field, The Ether Field, The Divine Matrix, The Divine Mind of God, or whatever one chooses to name It. It is what God sees and knows.

Monetary Reform as an issue represents a supreme opportunity for real leaders to choose which of the above versions of history they would want to have recorded as their permanent real legacy. The choice is whether or not to align with moral right the Founding Fathers envisioned for America.

4) To achieve this state of affairs, we support non-violent methods and solutions of civil disobedience in support of the constitutional provisions for money issuance and management and alignment with such personages as Henry David Thoreau, Mahatma Gandhi, and Dr. Martin Luther King. Simply reserve the right to refuse to elect or support **any** sitting or potential representative to Congress or the Senate unless he or she recognizes and acknowledges the seriousness of the problem and will vow to actively work to correct it. Follow through by conveying that you are serious about this issue and he or she should be also.

5) American citizens must ask politicians and the media these hard moral questions and demand truthful answers from them: **Why should America's money system belong to private bankers, who alone benefit from it? Why do you allow it to perpetuate? Should you not champion this cause?**

6) **Insist on public disclosure from all elected/potential representatives and newspaper editors as to where they stand on this issue of monetary reform. Write letters to the editor of the local newspapers**. Remember that a refusal to publish is information itself.

7) Finally, encourage everyone to do his or her own research in libraries and the Internet. Use a good Internet search engine such as Google, Yahoo, Ask.com, Ask Jeeves, or a host of others, and enter the phrase "Federal Reserve Conspiracy." There is an amazing wealth of documentation and information on this subject and issues to be found there. Using *Google* to search this phrase recently yielded nearly two million links! Also on Google, watch the videos "America—Freedom to Facism"

by Aaron Russo, "Fiat Empire, and "End Game: Blueprint for Global Enslavement" by Alex Jones." These exposés of the Federal Reserve and the Internal Revenue Service, although disturbing, are extremely enlightening in their detailing of the life we face if we do not restore the banking laws to conform to the Constitution.

Many people are justifiably concerned and are now engaged in contributing to this documentation and grass roots educational campaign. **We need you and everyone you know to get involved now.** It is truly amazing just how much information can be obtained on this subject now for those who choose to get interested.

We urge all Americans to write and call their respective congresspersons and senators and express the wish to have them restore the Constitution to its monetary provision. Withdraw your support if they will not do so. Encourage all people you know to educate themselves about the facts of this issue through the recommended texts and other sources. Get extra copies of this publication from Amazon.com or the authors to share with your family, friends, and associates this vitally important information of our possibilities for true freedom.

Choose to **get involved and expect positive change.** What we can expect is from *Debt Virus*:

Money will be available at all times, at low interest rates.

Business activity will be continuous, and employment will be available for those willing and available for work.

Economic growth will be limited only by imagination.

Inflation will never be reduced to zero as long as humankind suffers from greed, but its march will be severely hampered, thus protecting wages and savings.

Bankruptcies, foreclosures, business failures, and unemployment will no longer be tools used to balance prosperity.

It will no longer be impossible to repay the total private debt.

Prices will diminish along with debt and stabilize when debt is payable.

Boom and bust cycles will permanently disappear.

All debt held at the current time, both by the public and private sector, will fall and reach a level below that of the money supply.

Interest will no longer grow into an ever-increasing, unpayable debt.

Government borrowing will cease because it will no longer be necessary; taxation will drastically decline, and government can phase out the Internal Revenue Service.

Public debt can be reduced to zero, with governments earning interest on account balances rather than paying interest on debt.

All working people will be able to afford homes and cars and can save to enjoy comfortable and dignified retirement without depending on handouts from the government.

Usury will be abolished; the banking industry will be like any other business in a truly free enterprise system, practicing competitive banking.

AMERICAN FREE PRESS   October 2001

CONCLUSION

We speak for the more than 300,000,000 people who are tired of the economic and political control of America.

It is ludicrous and absurd for a few thousand enormously wealthy individuals with their banking connections to have more power than 300 million plus Americans. Some of these obscenely wealthy bankers are not even American citizens. Our situation violates reason and is morally wrong. What exists is the essence of insanity. We speak for the millions of veterans, American heroes who sleep in foreign and domestic graves because of America's commitment to human decency and freedom. We intend to replace, by legislation, the bankers' control by abolishing the Federal Reserve as a private corporation, and having it and its function placed under the control of the United States Treasury where it belongs.

The false claims of the Money Power that debt-free money will not work is a total fabrication. Consider England's lack of a national debt for 500 years; by the American colonies' use of government issued debt-free money; by the Island of Guernsey being without a national debt since 1822; by Lincoln's use of greenbacks to pay for the Civil War; and by Germany's use of debt-free money, which brought Germany back from the devastation of World War I to rebuild a great economy.

What the bankers mean by "won't work" is that they would no longer be able to collect nearly a trillion dollars yearly in interest on money created out of nothing. When America frees itself of the Money Power, other nations will follow our example, and the world will then become what the Founding Fathers envisioned for humankind. It will be a world of universal freedom, universal prosperity, and universal peace.

The last thing this world needs is a dictatorship, military or financial; a New World Order that is run by fascists. **The authors challenge anyone to disprove the facts and statements given here.** We hope that this information will spur Americans to action to throw off the Money Manipulators and take the fraud out of banking.

When the American people understand the proper function of government-issued debt-free money in our nation and act politically to secure it, this nation, under the moral right of God, will finally have a new birth of freedom and a government of the people, by the people, and for the people.

It is our hope that *Reality of Money and The Federal Reserve* has shown the reader the proper role of money in society as given in all the world's religions and by enlightened masters, sages, and philosophers.

Through such wise guidance, the correct moral choice regarding money becomes clear. All American citizens deserve to benefit, not just the bankers. We know on which side the bankers position themselves. Which will you choose?

In *Listen Humanity,* page133, Avatar Meher Baba reminds us:

The individual must fully understand his identity with the supreme universal Soul. Having perceived this truth, he will find that his life rearranges spontaneously so that his attitude towards his neighbor in everyday life becomes different. Then he will act upon the spiritual value of oneness, which promotes true cooperation.

May God help us all to aspire to and achieve this lofty but most worthy goal.

"The value of our dollar and the level of our interest rates are not supposed to be manipulated by the few members of the power elite meeting secretly in a marble palace. The Federal Reserve is unconstitutional, pure and simple. The only constitutional money is gold and silver, and notes redeemable in them. Not Fed funny money. Without the Federal Reserve, our money could not be inflated at the behest of big government or big banks. Your income and savings would not lose their value. Just as important, we wouldn't have this endless string of booms and busts, recessions and depressions, with each bust getting worse. They aren't natural to the free market; they're caused by the schemers at the Fed. President Andrew Jackson called the 19th century Fed "The Monster" because it was a vehicle for inflation and all sorts of special-interest corruption. Let me tell you, things haven't changed a bit. The record is a grim one and it was predicted by everyone who knew the inevitable results of giving politicians and central banks a printing press and letting them go hog-wild"

U.S. Representative Ron Paul, M.D., April 1998.

THE GOLDEN RULE IN WORLD RELIGIONS AND PHILOSOPHY

Our path to victory was built long ago. Wise people in many ages and in many parts of the world have come to the same conclusions regarding the most effective way to secure the best that is in people toward other people. The words they used to express the thought vary, though their meaning is the same. We call their conclusions *The Golden Rule*:

CHRISTIANITY: **Therefore all things whatsoever ye would that men should do to you, do you even so to them, for this is the laws and the prophets.** Matthew 7:12 King James Version

JUDAISM: **What is hateful to you, do not to your fellow men. That is the entire law; all the rest is commentary.** Talmud, Shabbat 31a.**...thou shalt love thy neighbor as thyself.** Leviticus 19:18

ZOROASTRIANISM: **That nature alone is good which refrains from doing unto another whatsoever is not good for itself.** Dadistan-i-dinik 94:5

Whatever is disagreeable to yourself do not do unto others. Shatast-na-Shayast 13:29

TAOISM: **Regard your neighbor's gain as your own gain, and your neighbor's loss as your own loss.** T'ai Shang Kan Ying P'ien

The sage has no interest of his own, but takes the interests of the people as his own. He is kind to the kind; he is also kind to the unkind, for Virtue is kind. He is faithful to the faithful; he is also faithful to the unfaithful, for Virtue is faithful. Tao The Ching, Chapter 49

BRAHMANISM: **This is the sum of Dharma (duty): Do naught unto others which would cause you pain if done to you.** Mahabharata, 5:1517

BUDDHISM: **Hurt not others in ways that you yourself would find harmful.** Udana-Varga 5:18

…a state that is not pleasing or delightful to me, how could I inflict that upon another? Samyutta Nlkaya v. 353

CONFUCIANISM: **Surely it is the maxim of loving kindness; do not do unto others that you would not have them do unto you.** Analects 15:23

Tse-king asked, "Is there one word that can serve as a principle of conduct for life?' Confucius replied, 'It is the word "shu"—reciprocity. **Do not impose on others**

what you yourself do not desire. Doctrine of the Mean 13.3

Try your best to treat others as you would wish to be treated yourself, and you will find that this is the shortest way to benevolence. Mencius VII.A.4

HINDUISM: **This is the sum of duty: Do not do to others what would cause pain if done to you.** Mahabharata 5:1517

ANCIENT EGYPTIAN: **Do for one who may do for you, that you may cause him thus to do.** The Tale of the Eloquent Peasant, 109 – 110 Translated by R.B Parkinson. The original dates to 1970 to 1640 BCE and may be the earliest version ever written.

ISLAM: **None of you [truly] believes until he wishes for his brother what he wishes for himself.** Number 13 of Imam Al-Nawawi's Forty Hadiths

JAINISM: **Therefore, neither does he [a sage] cause violence to others nor does he make others do so.** Acaragansutra 5.101-2

In happiness and suffering, in joy and grief, we should regard all creatures as we regard our own self. Lord Mahavira, 24th Tirthankara

A man should wander about treating all creatures as he himself would be treated. Sutrakritanga 1.11.33

SUFISM: The basis of Sufism is consideration of the hearts and feelings of others. If you haven't the will to gladden someone's heart, then at least beware lest you hurt someone's heart, for on our path, no sin exists but this. Dr. Javad Nurbakhsh, Master of the Nimatullahi Sufi Order

SIKHISM: Compassion, mercy, and religion are the support of the entire world. Japji Sahib

Don't create enmity with anyone as God is within everyone. Guru Arjan Devji: AG 259

No one is my enemy, none a stranger, and everyone is my friend. Guru Arjan Devji : AG 1299

UNITARIAN: We affirm and promote respect for the interdependence of all existence of which we are a part. Unitarian principles.

YORUBA: (Nigeria) One going to take a pointed stick to pinch a baby bird should first try it on himself to see how it hurts.

BAHA' I: WORLD FAITH: Ascribe not to any soul that which thou wouldst not have ascribed to thee, and say not that which thou does not…Blessed is he who preferreth his brother before himself. Baha'ullah

And if thine eyes be turned towards justice, choose thou for thy neighbor that which thou choosest for thyself. Epistle to the Son of the Wolf

HUMANISM: (5) Humanists acknowledge human interdependence, the need for mutual respect, and the kinship of all humanity.

(11) Humanists affirm that individual and social problems can only be resolved by means of human reason, intelligent effort, critical thinking joined with compassion and a spirit of empathy for all living beings.

NATIVE AMERICAN SPIRITUALITY: Respect for all life is the foundation. The Great Law of Peace

All things are our relatives: what we do to everything, we do to ourselves. All is really one. Black Elk

Do not wrong or hate your neighbor. For it is not he whom you wrong, but yourself. Pima Proverb

ROMAN PAGAN RELIGION: The law imprinted on the hearts of all men is to love the members of society as themselves.

SHINTO: **The heart of the person before you is a mirror. See there your own form...Be charitable to all beings, love is the representative of God.** Ko-ji-ki Hachiman Kasuga

WICCA: **An it harm no one, do what thou wilt.** (Do whatever you will, as long as it harms nobody, including yourself.) One's will is to be carefully thought out in advance of action. This is called the "Wiccan Rede."

SAGE'S/PHILOSOPHER'S GOLDEN RULE QUOTATIONS

EPICITUS, Circa 100CE: What you would avoid suffering yourself, seek not to impose on others.

KANT: Act as if the maxim of thy action were to become by thy will a universal law of nature.

PLATO, 4th century BC, Greece: May I do unto others as I would that they should do unto me.

SOCRATES, 5th century BCE: Do not do unto others that which would anger you if others did it to you.

SENECA, Epistle 47:11 Rome 1st century CE: Treat your inferiors as you would be treated by your superiors.

THE DALAI LAMA: Every religion emphasizes human improvement, love, respect for others, sharing other people's suffering. On these lines every religion had more or less the same viewpoint and the same goal.

MEHER BABA, 1894 – 1969: If we understand and feel that the greatest act of devotion and worship to

God is not to hurt or harm any of His beings, we are loving God. *How to Love God*, Sheriar Press

The only real knowledge is the knowledge that God is the inner dweller in good people and in so-called bad, in saint and in so-called sinner. This knowledge requires you to help all equally as circumstances demand without expectation of reward; when compelled to act in a dispute, to act without the slightest trace of enmity or hatred; to try to make others happy with brotherly or sisterly feeling for each one; and to harm no one in thought, word, or deed—not even those who harm you. *Discourses*, by Meher Baba, Sheriar Foundation, 1995, page 1.

What these wise men and religions are saying is simple. **Do no harm to anyone.** These various versions of the Golden Rule in twenty-one world religions are also known as the Ethic of Reciprocity. The source is www.religioustolerance.org. The quotes by Meher Baba are copyrighted by the Avatar Meher Baba Perpetual Charitable Trust and used by permission of the Sheriar Foundation, Myrtle Beach, South Carolina. It should be noted that throughout his lifetime, Meher Baba had no personal politics and endorsed no political positions, but His profound and appropriate words speak volumes about how we should relate to and treat each other. We can accomplish this by applying the essence of the Golden Rule to the important arena of monetary policies so that all may benefit.

Readers should reflect upon and contemplate the meaning of all these amazingly similar, but equally profound statements. Is it a coincidence, or an awesome purposeful synchronicity? **Note that all of these statements communicate essentially the same message even though their authors were separated by thousands of years in time and by thousands of miles in geography.** This is indeed indicative of a Divine Infinite Intelligence called God behind all forms in Nature and Existence, who cyclically and periodically dispenses wisdom from His eternal fountain. From the enlightened through the ages, it is disbursed widely to guide humanity to higher understanding between self and others, so that we may achieve lasting peace through cooperation, and receive His bountiful blessings of shelter and sustenance.

"The greatest monopoly in this country is the Money Monopoly. As long as it exists, true freedom, and the divine right to fully enjoy the fruits of one's labors will be non-existent. The money creators, through ignorance or design, have withheld the true facts about money from the public and their actions serve to dispossess humankind of wealth, property and freedom."

Jacques S. Jaikaran, M.D., Debt Virus.

FAMOUS QUOTATIONS

Edward Bulwer Lytton 1839: The pen is mightier than the sword, but the purse conquereth them both.

Greek poet Euripides circa 406 BC: The tongue is mightier than the blade.

Thomas Jefferson in a letter to Thomas Paine, 1796: Go on doing with your pen what in other times was done with the sword.

Shakespeare, 1600: …many wearing rapiers are afraid of goose quills.

Amshel Meyer Rothschild: Permit me to issue and control the money of a nation, and I care not who writes its laws.

Minnesota Congressman Charles A. Lindberg (father of the famous flyer) speaking in Congress about the Federal Reserve Act of 1913: When the President signs this bill, the invisible government will be legalized.

President Woodrow Wilson, in 1916 after he signed the Federal Reserve Act into law: I am a most unhappy man. Unwittingly, I have ruined my country.

Aristotle, Ethics 1133: Money exists not by nature but by law.

Henry David Thoreau: Rather than love or money or fame, give me truth.

Mahatma Gandhi: First they ignore you, then they laugh at you, then they fight you, then you win.

Old saying, unknown author: Let us not fight against evil, let us fight for what is good.

US Senator Louis T. McFadden, Chairman US Banking and Currency Commission for twenty-two years: The Federal Reserve (privately owned banks) is one of the most corrupt institutions the world has ever seen.

Sir Josiah Stamp, president of the Bank of England in an informal talk to students at the University of Texas, 1920: Banking was conceived in iniquity and born in sin...Bankers own the world...**If you want to continue to be the slaves of bankers, and pay the cost of your own slavery, let them continue to create money.**

5 USC 3331, the Congressional oath of office: I do solemnly swear that I will support the Constitution of the United States against all enemies, foreign and domestic; that I will bear true faith and allegiance to the same; that I will take this obligation freely, without any mental reservation or purpose of evasion, and that I will well and faithfully discharge the duties of the office on which I am about to enter. So help me God.

Exodus 20:13, the Eighth Commandment: **Thou shalt not steal.**

"He who passively accepts evil is as much involved in it as he who helps to perpetrate it. He who accepts evil without protesting against it is really cooperating with it."

Dr. Martin Luther King Jr., Stride Toward Freedom, 1958.

ABOUT US - THE AUTHORS

Frank Wallace:

At eighty-nine years of age, and understanding how and why America was founded, and how and why it grew to greatness, I am thoroughly disgusted with the American people for allowing the travesty and injustice of **our unlawful monetary policy of the Federal Reserve** to go on so long. This includes you and me and all of us.

I began writing about bringing down communism in the 1970s and was the founder and president of the Foundation to End Totalitarianism. After the fall of the Berlin Wall, I began a study of the monetary system in America.

I am a veteran of World War II, serving as an army supply officer, and I served in the Korean War as a captain, also as a supply officer. I have a BA and an MA in history from Mississippi College, served as a research and information director of the State Civil War Centennial Commission, and taught history and government at Gulf Coast Military Academy. I also was employed in the Research and Development Division of the Mississippi State Highway Department.

From my retirement in 1980, I have occupied myself with writing and speaking on national defense, foreign policy, and Federal Reserve issues with over twenty publications, and consider myself a practical idealist.

In this book, Stephen Clark and I hope to convince you to become fully informed about our economic situation and also the possibilities for yourself and your children and grandchildren and our beloved country.

Stephen Clark:

Even from adolescence, I strongly suspected there was something very wrong with our society, but could not then quite grasp the cause. Being a natural seeker of truth and having an inquisitive mind, I eventually discovered the prime reason for our increasingly dysfunctional society was the application by selfish and spiritually ignorant people, of immoral monetary banking laws due to their ability to dominate unfairly through undeserved power.

I am a veteran of the Vietnam Era, serving in the US Coast Guard from 1967 to 1973, including two years of inactive reserve duty as a quartermaster/signalman, and was honorably discharged in 1971 as an E-6. I eventually earned a degree in marine science from Cape Fear Technical Institute and became employed with the US Naval Oceanographic Office as a scientist in 1978, traveling and working in many countries around the world. I retired in 2003 as GS-12/9, after nearly thirty years as a public servant, including military service. As a senior scientist, I was involved in designing, planning, writing, compiling, and publishing technical specifications for supervising and conducting foreign hydrographic and oceanographic surveys.

A lifelong interest is being a self-taught musician, for over forty years, playing guitar and singing folk-country-rock songs of social consciousness. I also write songs, poetry, and research, investigate, and write about consciousness, ancient and alternative history.

These experiences, combined with a lifetime investigation of the spiritual truths through the mystics in the various world religions and philosophy, prepared me to eventually discover that the main cause of social injustice in our era, was that in the 1700s, 1800s, and early 1900s, selfish, cruel and greedy people were very active and successful in putting themselves in charge of our world governments, and of subverting the monetary provisions of the US Constitution, mainly through financial subterfuge.

Self-interest and ignorance of spiritual truth is the real cause of all our collective problems. Small, but extremely powerful groups of self-interested individuals long ago managed to capture the secrets of monetary creation in order to exploit the vast human population to satisfy their own greed.

BIBLIOGRAPHY – RECOMMENDED READING

Aristotle, On Man In The Universe. Walter J. Black, Inc. for the Classics Club, 1943

Benham, Dan. *A Phone Call to the Fed,* d.benham@worldnet.att.net, 2002

Bradley, Michael. *Secrets of the Freemasons,* Barnes & Noble, 2006

Coogan, Gertrude M. *Money Creators,* Omni Publications, 1935

Cook, Peter. *The Credit Money Bluebook,* Monetary Science Publishing, 1990

Cook, Peter. *Modern Money Mechanics: Capitalism, Socialism For Bankers,* Monetary Science Publishing

Cook, Peter. *AWESOME POWERS OF: BANK DEPOSIT MONEY,* Monetary Science Publishing, 1997

Edson, Steve, CDR, US Navy (ret.), Letter to the Editor, *Sun Herald,* Biloxi, Mississippi, May 15, 2003

Elletson, Roger E. Self-published March, 1985 Bulletin: *Legacy to the Victims of Corporate America*

Emry, Sheldon. "Billions for the Bankers: Debts for the People," *American Free Press*, Special Reprint of a Classic Report by Sheldon Emry

Ewart, James E. *Money*, Principia Publishing, Inc., 1998

Griffin, Edward G. *The Creature from Jekyll Island: A Second Look at the Federal Reserve*, American Media, 1994

Helsing, Jan van. *Secret Societies and Their Power in the 20th Century*, EWERTVERLAG, 1995

Hemphill, Robert H. *Senate Document #23, 76th Congress 1st Session*

Icke, David. *…and the truth shall set you free*, Bridge of Love Publications, 1995

Jaikaran, Jacques, MD. *Debt Virus*, Glenridge Publishing

Lindberg, Charles A. *Lindberg on the Federal Reserve*, (Formerly titled *The Economic Pinch*) The Noontide Press, 1923

Marrs, Jim. *Rule by Secrecy*, Harper Collins, 2000

Monetary Science Publications. "Bankernomics in One Easy Lesson – The Bankers Manifesto,"

Media By-Pass Magazine, Evansville, Indiana

Meher Baba. *Discourses,* Sheriar Foundation, 1995

Meher Baba. *Listen Humanity,* Crossroads Publishing Co., 1998

Morehead, Philip. The Penguin's Roget's Thesaurus in Dictionary Form, Penguin Reference

Mullins, Eustace. *The Federal Reserve Conspiracy,* OMNI Publications, 1971

Ontario Consultants of Religious Tolerance, "Shared belief in the 'Golden Rule' (aka Ethics of Reciprocity) Versions of the Golden Rule in 21 World Religions," www.religioustolerance.org

Perkins, John. *Confessions of an Economic Hit Man,* Plume. Penguin Group Inc. authorized reprint published by: Berrett-Koehler Publishers, Inc., 2004

Porter, Thomas. *The Green Magicians,* OMNI Publications, 1968

Quigley, Carroll. *Tragedy and Hope: A History of the World in Our Time*, GSG & Associates Publishing, P.O. Box 590 San Pedro, CA 90733

Snow, Anthony. Letters to the Editor, *American Free Press*

The Sun Herald, Biloxi, MS

Vieira, Dr. Edwin Jr., *The Federal Reserve Banking System: Fatal Parasite on the American Body Politic*, http://home.hiwaay.net/~becraft/VieiraMono4.htm

Wallace, Frank. *There Is a Way*, self-published, 1957

Weekly World News

Wickliffe, Vennard B. Sr. *The Federal Reserve Hoax: The Age Of Deception*, Tenth Ed., 1967, Forum Publishing Co.

Zarlenga, Stephen. *The Lost Science of Money: The Mythology of Money – the Story of Power*, American Monetary Institute Charitable Trust, 2002

Zarlenga, Stephen. *The American Money Scene*, American Monetary Institute, 2006

"**Reality of Money and The Federal Reserve** is a bold and compelling narrative that will surely awaken the reader to the usury swindles perpetuated by the Federal Reserve Banks, a private corporation that is no part of our government. Stephen Clark and Frank Wallace are to be commended for their dauntless research into the constitutional failure, corruption, and deteriorating monetary system all Americans now endure."

George S. Gabric, GSG & Associates, San Pedro, CA, Publishers of *Tragedy And Hope: A History of The World In Our Time*, *The Evolution Of Civilization: An Introduction to Historical/Political Analysis*, and *The Anglo-American Establishment*, all titles by the late Georgetown University history professor, Carroll Quigley

Made in the USA
Charleston, SC
15 June 2010